A Williamson's Book

Kids Make Magic!

The Complete G   **zing Magician**

Library of Congress Cataloging-in-Publication Data

Burgess, Ron.
    Kids make magic! : the complete guide to becoming an amazing magician / Ron Burgess.
       p. cm. -- (Kids can!)
    Includes index.
    Summary: Offers guidelines and tips for putting together a magic act including selecting a wand, mastering official terminology, developing a stage personality, and selecting and performing tricks.
    ISBN 1-885593-87-2
    1. Magic tricks--Juvenile literature. [1. Magic tricks.] I. Title. II. Series

GV1548.B87 2003
793.8--dc21

                                                              2003043091

Kids Can!® series editor: **Susan Williamson**   Cover design: **Marie Ferrante-Doyle**
Project editor: **Vicky Congdon**   Cover illustrations: **Michael Kline**
Interior design: **Dana Pierson**   Cover photography: **Karen Pike**
Interior decorative illustrations: **Sarah Rakitin**   Printing: **Capital City Press**
Interior technical illustrations: **Marie Ferrante-Doyle**

Williamson Publishing Co.
P.O. Box 185
Charlotte, VT 05445
(800) 234-8791

Printed in the United States

10 9 8 7 6 5 4 3 2 1

Kids Can!®, *Little Hands*®, *Quick Starts for Kids!*®, *Kaleidoscope Kids*®, and *Tales Alive!*® are registered trademarks of Williamson Publishing.

Good Times™ and *You Can Do It!*™ are trademarks of Williamson Publishing.

Dedication

To my loving wife, Louise, our five children, and our eight grandchildren, especially our newest, Nicholas David Bottone.

Acknowledgments

I'm truly grateful to the staff of Williamson Publishing for all the help and guidance, not only with this book, but also with my other books that they have published as well. I would list all of their names but I probably would leave someone out. So to all of you, thank you very much.

Also by Ron Burgess

YO-YO!
Tips & Tricks
from a Pro

BE A CLOWN!
Techniques from
a Real Clown

Contents

abracadabra!

allakazam!

Can I Really Be a Magician?

Magic is making people believe you can do the impossible. Of course you can't really do the impossible, but you can make people think you did. And magic tricks are performed to entertain, to amuse, or to challenge people to think, the way a good puzzle does.

Magic tricks are not hard to do. Some tricks happen almost by themselves, just by the way you hold, bend, or fold the item. Even the most elaborate trick that you see on television probably has a very simple explanation. In that sense, anyone can do magic. It's not that some people are born with special powers. Just as with any skill, your magic is created with preparation, planning, and practice.

I've grouped the tricks in this book by type: card tricks, coin tricks, rope tricks, etc. You can start with any kind of trick you want to perform, but I do recommend that you learn the tricks in the order they are presented within each chapter. In some cases, the tricks do get a little more involved as you move through the chapter and there may be steps or movements in the beginning tricks that will help you learn the tricks that follow.

So, yes, you *can* be a magician! The point of magic is fun and enjoyment for you and for your audience. So, relax! Smile! And on with the show!

Ron Burgess

What Every Magician Needs to Know

Welcome to the world of the magician — a world of mysterious illusions, wacky words, and make-believe fun! Before you jump right into practicing tricks, however, there are some basics about performing magic you'll need to know. Here I'll help you put together a vocabulary of magic words and show you how to talk your way through a trick. So, Presto! Let's go!

The Three Basic Rules of Magic

Each magician has his own rules for performing magic and for doing specific tricks, but I'm sure every magician will agree on these three basic rules of magic.

- Never tell how a trick is done.
- Practice, practice, and then practice some more.
- Never repeat a trick.

Never tell how a trick is done

Magicians have a code of honor to never give out the secret behind a trick. So before you go any further, I want you to put your left hand on this book, raise your right hand and say, "I will never, ever tell anyone how a trick is done."

If you tell people how a trick works, they see how easy and simple it was and then they're embarrassed that they were stumped by something so obvious. "Boy, that's stupid," they'll say, "That's not even a trick." Deep in our hearts we all know people can't really do magic but it's fun to imagine it might be possible. It's like seeing a sci-fi movie or reading an improbable tale. You know it isn't true and couldn't happen, but you suspend belief and you are entertained. And that is what magic is — entertainment. So don't tell and people will be entertained.

Practice, practice, and then practice some more

This is what all magicians do and will tell you to do. Practice every chance you get. A lot of short practice periods are better than a couple of long ones. See HOW TO PRACTICE A NEW TRICK (page 11) for more tips.

Ssshhhhh!

Never repeat a trick

At least, don't repeat the same trick to the same people on the same day. Your audience will know what the ending is, so they'll be examining you and the trick more closely, looking for the secret. If someone says, "Do that again," you can say, "Here's another trick with a rope (or a scarf or whatever) that you might like" and move smoothly on to the next trick. After a while people will forget the details of a trick so you can eventually do it again.

How Much Does Being a Magician Cost?

Magic can cost as little or as much as you want to spend. Professional magicians buy really elaborate tricks for thousands of dollars. The inexpensive tricks described in this book let you discover which types of tricks you prefer doing. Once you get good at these tricks, you can check the library or bookstores for books with more advanced tricks. Then you could buy a few small tricks from a magic store. If you have a magic store near you, the salespeople are always happy to show you how a trick is performed. Check out RESOURCES (pages 123–124).

Just Say the Magic Word!

To make your magic happen, you have to do something, like snap your fingers, clap your hands, or wave your magic wand, and, of course, say some magic words. It's all part of the illusion of magic, and it alerts your audience to the change that's about to take place. Try different ones and see what works for you.

Traditional magic words: Abracadabra, Hocus Pocus, Presto, Allakazam

with some variations: Presto Change-O and Hocus Pocus Domino-cus.

Rhyming magic words: "Hocus Pocus Allakazoo. Make this handkerchief turn to blue."

Mixed-up magic words: "Have a Banana" for Abracadabra or "Hokey Pokey" for Hocus Pocus. (The audience will surely let you know that you're saying it wrong!)

Your own funny magic words: Purple Pickled Prunes, Wicky Wacky Winkle, Lollapaloosa, Kowabunga, Shazam.

shazam!

Keep That Patter Going!

Patter is the steady stream of words you say while you are doing each step of the trick to distract the audience or direct them to what they should be focusing on. Throughout the book, I've included some very simple patter for most of the tricks just to get you started. Practice the trick to learn it well and then work on your own patter. Make up a funny story around the trick, tell a made-up version of the history of the trick, or just explain what the audience needs to know, or what they should be watching.

HOCUS POCUS Allakazoo!

meow!

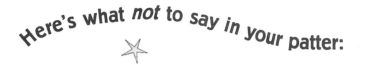

 Avoid telling the audience what it already knows or can see: "Here I have an empty bag" or "This is a perfectly ordinary piece of rope." When you say things that are really obvious, the audience gets suspicious and starts examining everything more closely.

 Don't say what you are going to do in advance as in "I will now change this handkerchief from red to green" or "This five of hearts will jump from the deck into my right pocket." You spoil the surprise and again, you will make people suspicious.

 Don't use someone else's patter (well, of course you can use my simple patter from this book to get started) or tell stories that are obviously not true; you want the audience to trust you. Write your own patter and be original!

 If you want to tell a story while you're doing a trick, don't try to make it up as you are doing the trick. Plan the story out in advance and write it all down. Practice the trick with the patter. Make changes and corrections. Once you have the trick and the patter down correctly, then it's OK to improvise by changing a word or two as you go along.

 Skip the long, drawn-out stories or jokes. You'll bore the audience and they'll stop paying attention. Remember the word KISS: Keep It Short and Simple. (If you want to toss a few short magician jokes into your routine, see page 119).

Emphasize the obvious! *That's what makes all magic "work." The people watching you won't be looking for anything unusual, and there are a lot of things they won't notice unless you point them out — so don't! Instead, remind them of what's obvious. When you pick up a section of trick newspaper, for example, rather than saying "Now there's nothing hidden in this newspaper," you might say, "I haven't read today's paper yet. Let's see what it says."*

Misdirection

You don't have to use any quick or fancy maneuvers to do a trick but sometimes you will need to direct the audience's attention to something else so you can do a secret move. That's called *misdirection*.

Here are some ways to make the audience look away from what you are about to do. Once you start practicing and get used to doing magic, you'll find your own ways to use misdirection and patter in your act.

* If you hold something up in your right hand and look at it, people will tend to look at your right hand. That leaves you free to do something with your left hand.

* If you take something from your left hand with your right hand and you tell people that's what you're doing ("So I'm passing this coin from one hand to the other"), they will believe what they "see" and what you told them. But what you are actually doing is keeping the coin hidden in your left palm and only pretending to take the coin with your right hand.

* If you look right at the people watching, they will tend to look back at you. If you look at a prop, the audience will look at the prop. Both of these misdirections will give you just enough time to do something or hide something where people aren't looking.

* If you repeat an action two or three times, the audience will stop paying close attention and you can do your secret move. Also, a loud noise, like a foot stomping, will temporarily distract the audience's attention.

How to Practice a New Trick

Here's an easy way to add a new trick to your routine.

1. Think about how you want to present the trick and plan what to say as you're performing each step (JUST SAY THE MAGIC WORD!, page 8). Write out a script.

2. Practice the trick in front of a mirror while saying the words. This way you can see how the trick looks to your audience. Make changes and practice again.

3. Once you have the trick perfected, practice in front of your baby brother or sister or your cat or dog to get the feeling of performing in front of an audience. Then practice it in front of your mom or dad or your best friend.

Magic Wands

Your magic wand is one of the most important parts of your act! Sure, you can do all these tricks without one, but a wand adds pizzazz to your presentation.

You can buy many different types of magic wands at magic shops — from breakaway wands (they fall apart when someone holds them) to stretching wands to wands that change color or turn into a bouquet of flowers. Or you can easily make your own one-of-a-kind version. The key thing is to choose a wand that works for you and your act and to practice so that you feel comfortable performing tricks with it.

Making a Wand

The best thing about wands is that you can make many of them yourself. Here are two to consider.

Traditional Magic Wand

You need: ¹/2" (1 cm) diameter wooden dowel about 10" to 12" (25 to 30 cm) long; white and black tempera paints, small paintbrush

To make the wand:

Paint 1" (2.5 cm) of each end white.
Paint the rest of the dowel black.

Fancy Magic Wand

You need: ¹/2" (1 cm) diameter wooden dowel about 10" to 12" (25 to 30 cm) long, colorful tempera paints, small paintbrush, star-shaped stickers, glitter and glue

To make the wand:

Paint the ends of the wand gold or silver and the body a bright color like red or purple. Or, the wand could have red and white stripes like a candy cane. Cover it with stars or glitter. You could even make a large cardboard star for the end.
The possibilities are endless.

Simple Wand Tricks

Let's try some simple tricks so that you can practice using your new wand!

✳ Which Finger is Which? ✳

Throughout the book, I'll refer to your fingers as follows:

THUMBS

LEFT   RIGHT

I wrote the instructions for all of these tricks for a right-handed person. If it's more comfortable to switch hands and use the opposite ones from what I've described and shown, go for it! Tricks are most convincing when they are performed confidently and gracefully, so do whatever is easiest.

Floating Magic Wand Trick

The magic: You make a wand float in midair.

Props: wand, piece of black thread, pencil, wristwatch

Preparation: Tie the thread to the wand between the two end tips. Place a pencil under your wristwatch band on your left hand.

THE THREAD IS JUST LOOSE ENOUGH TO SLIP YOUR HAND THROUGH

The trick:

1. Show your magic wand and show that both hands are empty.

2. Turn the left side of your body toward the audience. Hold your left arm up in front of you with your left hand wide open and the back of your hand facing the audience.

3. *"And now, the floating magic wand trick."*

   Place the wand in your left hand and close your fist around it.

4. Slowly open your left hand, and the wand will fall to the floor. Pick it up.

5. *"Let's try that again. I'll have to steady my arm."*

   Hold your left wrist with your right hand to steady it.

   Secretly put the first finger of your right hand on the wand and press it to your left hand.

6. *"Stay!"*

   Slowly open your left hand and the wand stays in midair.

SECRETLY HOLD THE WAND WITH YOUR FIRST FINGER

WHAT THE AUDIENCE SEES

7. *"Move up! (or down)."*

Move the first finger of your right hand up and down, and the wand looks as if it is moving.

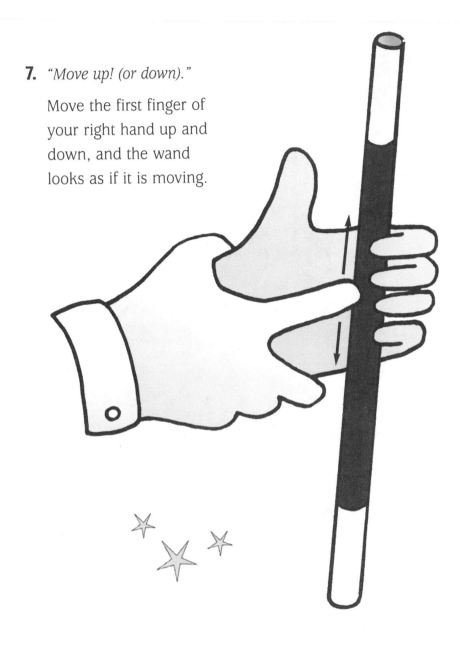

8. *"Fall!"*

Let go with your finger, and the wand falls to the floor.

9. *"OK. Does anyone know how that trick is done? Right! I use my finger."*

Hold the wand again with the first finger of your right hand and turn your left hand around so the audience can see.

10. *"So that's how you do it."*

Turn your left hand back around.

This time, however, secretly pull out the pencil that you have hidden under your wristwatch band and slide it over the wand.

11. *"But if you are a real magician, you can ..."*

Slowly remove your right hand from your left wrist.

"... remove your hand."

The wand stays in midair, supported by the pencil.

12. *"OK, I fooled you again. See, I had the pencil holding the wand."*

Show the audience.

13. *"Let me show you how to do that with my hand facing you."*

Remove the wand from under the pencil. With your palm facing the audience, secretly slide the fingers of your left hand through the black thread on the wand.

Slide the wand under the pencil.

14. *"Now here's the best part of this trick. You can even take away the pencil ..."*

Pull the pencil out.

" ... and the wand still stays there."

bravo!

Wand in the Mail Trick

The magic: You make a full-size magic wand appear from a small envelope.

Props: letter-size envelope with address and cancelled stamp on it, magic wand

Preparation: Make a slit in the bottom of the envelope. Hide your wand up your left sleeve.

The trick:

1. *"Everyone always wonders where magicians get their magic wands."*

   Pick up the envelope with your right hand and show it to the audience.

2. *"Well, we usually get them in the mail."*

   Transfer the envelope to your left hand and with your thumb, push the tip of the wand into the slit on the envelope. Your fingers on the outside of the envelope will hide what you are doing.

3. Reach into the envelope with your right hand and pull the magic wand through.

4. Discard the envelope to hide the evidence.

WHAT THE AUDIENCE SEES

Take a bow!

I even got my assistant in the mail!

Vanishing Wand Trick

The magic: You make a magic wand disappear and then reappear.

Props: magic wand, old newspaper, table, hollow wand (page 21)

Preparation: Hide the real magic wand in a place that allows you to retrieve it easily: behind your back, tucked into your pants or belt, in your inside coat pocket, in a box or bag on the table, or up your sleeve. Place a sheet of old newspaper on the table.

The trick:

1. Perform a trick like the WAND IN THE MAIL TRICK (page 18) using the hollow wand. When you're finished, place it on the newspaper.

2. *"OK, I won't need my magic wand anymore."*

   Roll up the fake wand in the newspaper. Say whatever magic words you like and tear up the newspaper. Discard the newspaper (with the fake wand inside). Wipe your hands clean.

3. *"Then again, I might need that magic wand for some other tricks."*

   Produce the real magic wand from where you have it hidden.

Making a Hollow Wand

You need: wooden dowel the same width as your magic wand, small handsaw (for use with adult help), white tempera paint, small paintbrush, glue, black construction paper

To make the wand:

1. Cut two pieces from the wooden dowel. Each piece should be 1" (2.5 cm) longer than the white tips of the real magic wand. Paint both cut pieces white to match the real wand. Let dry.

2. Glue the construction paper around the black part of the real magic wand so that it makes a "shell" that you can slide on and off the real wand.

3. Glue the two white wooden tips inside the black construction-paper shell, making the hollow wand the same length as the real one.

LOOKS JUST LIKE THE REAL THING!

Tricks Using Odds & Ends

Most of the magicians you see on TV perform very elaborate tricks that cost hundreds of dollars. Did you know you can perform some great tricks using odds and ends you have lying around the house? It doesn't take a big production to make a trick good; smooth moves and an entertaining delivery will do it. Some of the following tricks are just as mystifying as the big flashy ones. In fact, I've seen the professional magicians David Copperfield, Lance Burton, and David Blaine do one or two of these on TV, so you're in good company! For more tricks using odds and ends like spoons and other eating utensils, see pages 83 to 90.

Crayon Trick

The magic: A person chooses a crayon. You correctly guess the color without seeing the crayon.

Prop: box of eight crayons

The trick:

1. *"I'm going to turn my back. I want you to open the box of crayons, pick one and put it in my right hand. Then close the box so I won't be able to see what crayon you've selected."*

When the person has done that, turn back around but keep your hands behind your back.

2. While your hands are behind your back, make a small mark on your left thumbnail with the crayon. Make a loose fist with your left hand and bring it out in front of you. Keep the thumbnail facing you. Take a very quick, secret peek at it as you bring it around and then hide it in the fist. Be sure to practice this step, because it's important to do it in one fluid motion. Keep the crayon behind your back.

3. *"I want you to concentrate on the color you selected. The color you selected is blue."* (or whatever it was).

Bring the crayon out and display it.

Candy Machine Trick

The magic: You dispense candy from an empty candy machine.

Props: small pieces of wrapped candy like chocolate kisses, empty film canister labeled Magic Candy Machine

Preparation: Place the candy in your right pocket and the canister on top.

The trick:

1. *"Would you like some candy?"*

   Pull the canister and a piece of candy from your pocket with your right hand. The piece of candy should be against your right palm and the canister should be in front of it. As you curl your hand around the canister, it will hide the piece of candy behind it.

2. *"This is my new candy machine that I just invented. You start with an empty container."*

   With your left hand, take the lid off of the canister to show it's empty, then put the lid back on.

3. *"Hocus Pocus! Allakazam! Make some candy as quick as you can!"*

Take the lid off the empty canister and tip it into the person's hand. As you do, release the piece of candy you are hiding into her hand.

4. Put the canister back in your pocket quickly because you know someone else is going to want a piece of candy. Be ready to pull out the canister and another piece of candy.

allakazam!

Rubber Band Tricks

For all the rubber band tricks, use a 2" or 3" (5 to 7.5 cm) rubber band. If you use rubber bands that are longer or shorter, you'll have trouble with their movement. The thickness doesn't matter so much in terms of ease in doing the trick, but when you're performing in front of a big group of people, thick bands are easier for everyone to see.

Magical Mini-Routine

These rubber band tricks make a great mini-routine because you can move smoothly from one to the next. Then add a jumping paper clip (pages 31 to 32) for the finale!

Jumping Rubber-Band Trick

The magic: You make a rubber band jump from the first and second fingers to the third and fourth fingers of one hand — and then back again!

Prop: rubber band

The trick:

1. Place the rubber band over the first and second fingers of your left hand. The rubber band should be around the bases of the fingers. Hold your hand up with the back of your hand facing the audience and your palm facing you.

2. With the thumb and first finger of your right hand, pull the rubber band down toward the right of side your left hand.

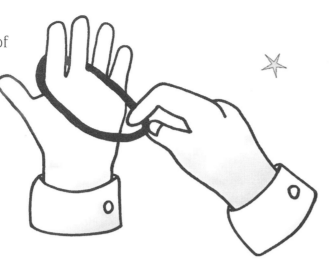

3. Curl the fingers of your left hand down toward your palm and place all four fingers into the rubber band. Let go of the rubber band with your right hand so it rests on the fingernails of your left hand.

4. Straighten up your fingers and the rubber band will jump to the third and fourth fingers.

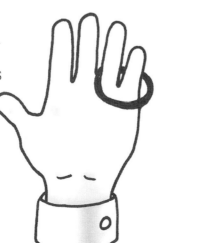

To send the rubber band back to your first and second fingers:

1. Hold up your left hand up again (the rubber band is around your third and fourth fingers).

2. With the first finger and thumb of your right hand, pull the rubber band down, this time to the *left* of your palm.

3. Curl the fingers of your left hand down toward your palm and place them in the rubber band. Let go of the rubber band with your right hand so it rests on the fingernails of your left hand.

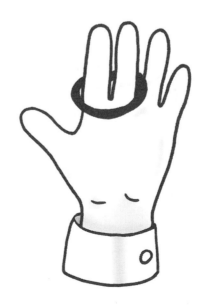

4. Straighten up your fingers and the rubber band will jump back to your first and second fingers.

Double Jumping Rubber-Band Trick

The magic: You make two rubber bands change places on the fingers of one hand.

Props: 2 different-colored rubber bands (tan and red, for example)

The trick:

1. Hold your left hand up with the back of your hand facing the audience and your palm facing you. Place the **tan** rubber band over the first and second fingers of your left hand.

2. Place the **red** rubber band over the third and fourth fingers of the same hand. Both rubber bands should be around the bases of your fingers.

3. With the thumb and first finger of your right hand, pull the **red** rubber band to the left side of your left hand and place it over your left thumb.

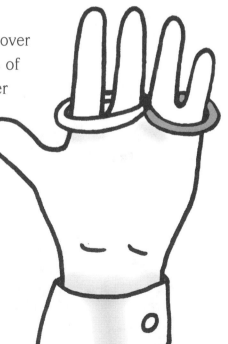

4. Pull the **tan** rubber band over the **red** band and down to the right side of your palm.

5. Curl the fingers of your left hand down and place them into the opening where the two rubber bands cross.

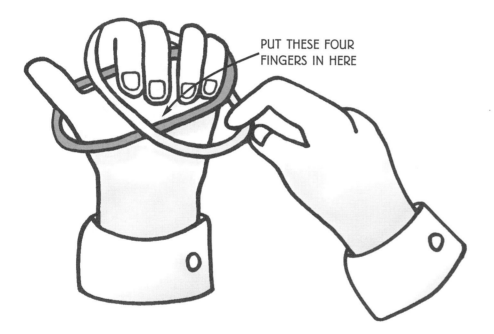

PUT THESE FOUR FINGERS IN HERE

6. Let go of the **tan** rubber band with your right hand and it will rest on the fingernails of your left hand. Pull out your thumb, and the **red** rubber band will rest on your fingernails with the **tan** rubber band.

7. *"And now the tan rubber band on my first two fingers and the red rubber band on my third and fourth fingers ... "*

Straighten up your fingers and the rubber bands will jump to the opposite fingers.

... will switch places!"

Impossible Rubber-Band Jump Trick

The magic: You make two rubber bands change places while a third one stays put, all on one hand.

Props: 3 different-colored rubber bands (tan, red, and green, for example)

The trick:

1. Place the **tan** and **red** rubber bands on your left hand as you did in steps 1 and 2 of the DOUBLE JUMPING RUBBER-BAND TRICK (page 28).

2. Twist the **green** rubber band over the tips of the four fingers of your left hand as shown.

OVER FIRST FINGER

TWIST

OVER SECOND FINGER

TWIST

OVER THIRD FINGER

TWIST

OVER FOURTH FINGER

3. Proceed with the DOUBLE JUMPING RUBBER-BAND TRICK from step 3. When you straighten your fingers, the **tan** and **red** rubber bands will have changed places and the **green** rubber band won't have moved.

Paper Clip & Double Jumping Rubber-Band Trick

The magic: You make a paper clip jump back and forth from the rubber bands on the fingers of one hand.

Props: paper clip, 2 identical (same size and same color) rubber bands

The trick:

1. Loop a paper clip onto one of the rubber bands.

2. Follow the instructions for the DOUBLE JUMPING RUBBER-BAND TRICK (page 28). It will look as if the paper clip jumped from one band to the other.

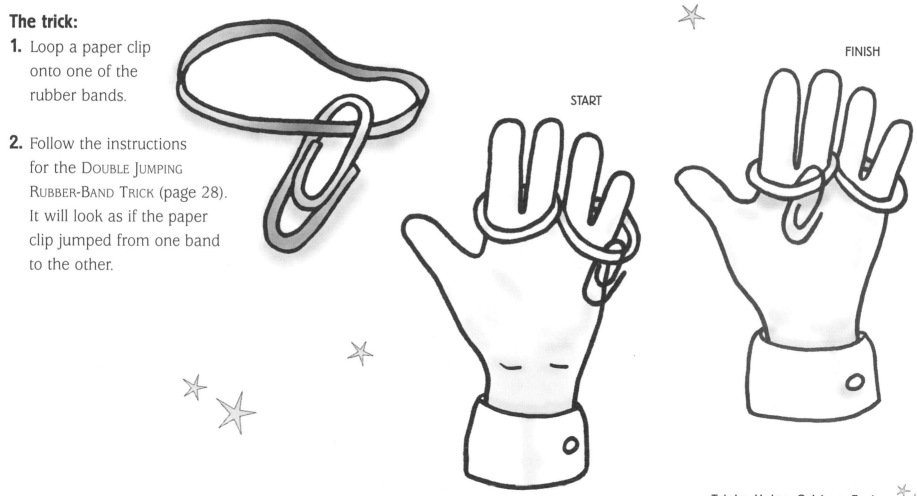

START

FINISH

3. If you use two different-colored rubber bands, the rubber band with the paper clip jumps.

START

FINISH

encore!

encore!

Tricks with Coins

I'm willing to bet that the first trick you ever saw was someone pulling a coin out of a person's ear (maybe even your own!). OK, so it's not an earth-shattering trick but everyone does it, including that very famous magician David Copperfield.

Coin magic is perfect for spur-of-the-moment tricks because everyone usually has a few coins handy. A quarter is just the right size for doing most coin tricks.

Coin from the Ear Trick

The magic: You pull a coin out of someone's ear.

Prop: coin

Preparation: Slip a coin into your right pocket.

 **Make it smooth!**
Practice this trick with another person (or even a stuffed animal with ears!) in front of a mirror until you can get right up close to the ear and make the motion look smooth and convincing.

The trick:

1. *"What's that I see there?"*

Look at someone's head or ear.

2. Of course he will say, "Where?" While talking and looking at the person, slip your right hand into your right pocket and bring out the coin. Use your thumb to hold the coin behind your first and second fingers. If you bend these fingers slightly as shown, it will hide the coin from the audience.

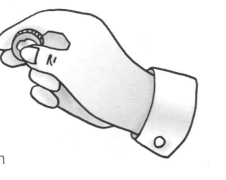

3. *"Right here behind your ear."*

Reach up to his ear with your right hand. As you pull your hand back, push the coin to your fingertips with your thumb. It looks as if you're pulling the coin from behind the person's ear.

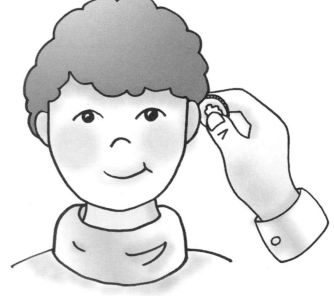

Coin Escapes from a Handkerchief Trick

The magic: You wrap a quarter up completely in a handkerchief and then slip it out without leaving a tear or a hole.

Props: quarter; handkerchief, bandanna, or silk scarf (MAGICIAN'S SILKS, page 72)

The trick:

1. *"A quarter doesn't like to be covered up."*

Hold up a quarter between the thumb and first finger of your left hand. With your right hand, drape the handkerchief over the quarter and your left hand. One point should face the audience and another point should rest on your arm.

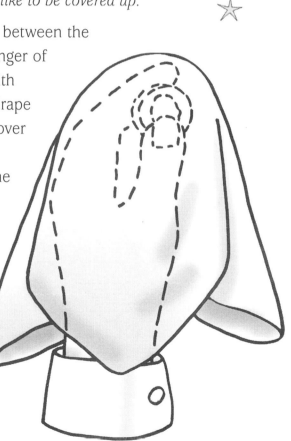

2. With your right hand, adjust the handkerchief so it's centered over the quarter. As you "fuss" with it, secretly pinch a small piece of the handkerchief between your left thumb and the quarter. This leaves a small pocket of cloth between your thumb and the quarter.

SMALL POCKET

SECRETLY PINCH HERE

3. *"It loves to be out in the sunlight."*

With your right hand, lift the front corner of the handkerchief that is facing the audience.

Pull it up completely over the quarter and all the way back to your left arm. This shows the quarter to the audience.

4. *"If you cover it over …"*

With your right hand, grab both ends of the handkerchief that are lying on your left arm and bring them up and forward over the quarter.

To the audience it looks as if you are covering the quarter, but what you're really doing is releasing the quarter from the handkerchief. (When you're first practicing this trick, if you want to check that the coin is loose from the handkerchief, peek underneath. You'll see the coin near your finger and the folded handkerchief near your thumb.)

5. Hold the quarter and handkerchief with the thumb and first finger of your right hand and take your left hand out from underneath the handkerchief.

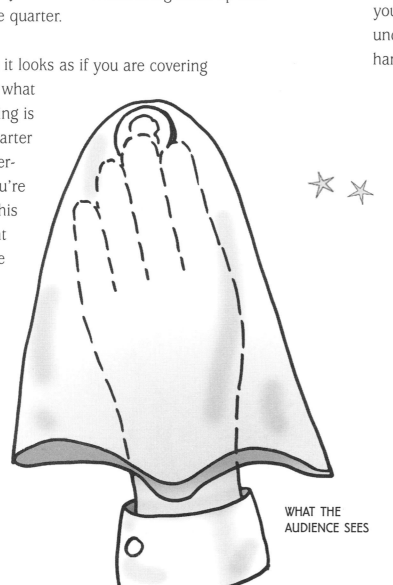

WHAT THE
AUDIENCE SEES

6. Hold the handkerchief about 2" (5 cm) down from the quarter with your left hand and continue pinching the quarter with the thumb and first finger of your right hand.

2" (5 CM)

7. Twist the handkerchief below the quarter so the audience can clearly see the shape of the quarter through the handkerchief.

8. *" ... it works its way out again ..."*

Hold the handkerchief in the twist with your left hand as you pretend to work the quarter up through the handkerchief with your right hand.

Pull the quarter completely out of the handkerchief and drop it on the table.

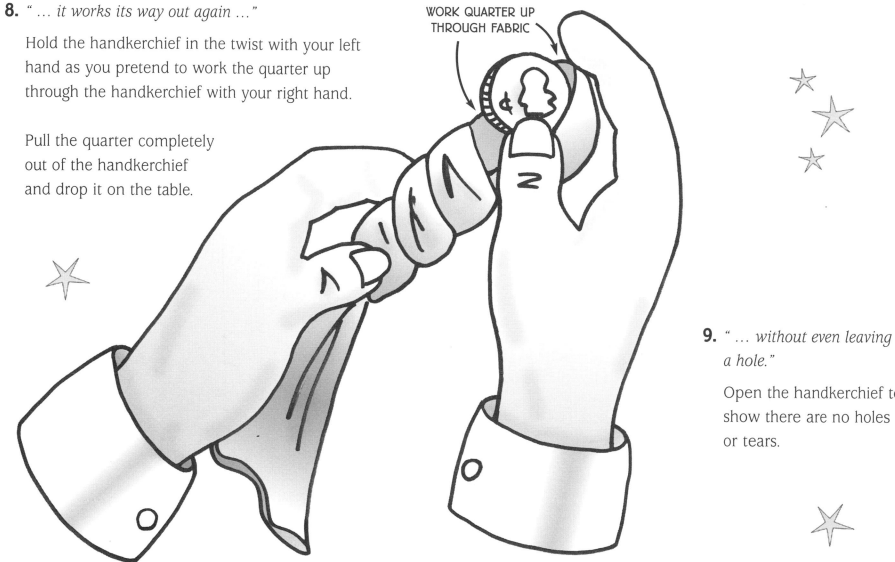

WORK QUARTER UP THROUGH FABRIC

9. *" ... without even leaving a hole."*

Open the handkerchief to show there are no holes or tears.

Fold Away the Coin Trick

The magic: You borrow a coin from your audience. You fold it up in a piece of paper, but when you rip up the paper, the coin is gone.

Prop: 3" X 5" (7.5 X 12.5 cm) piece of paper

The trick:

1. *"Sometimes I surprise myself with the tricks I do."*

Borrow a coin from someone. Hold the paper in your left hand, facing it toward the audience, with the 3" (7.5 cm) edge toward the floor. Hold the coin with the thumb and first finger of your right hand.

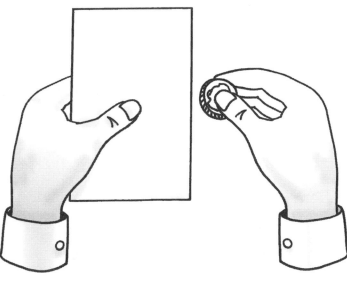

2. *"I really don't know how this trick is done."*

Place the coin against the paper as shown and hold it there with the first finger and thumb of your left hand.

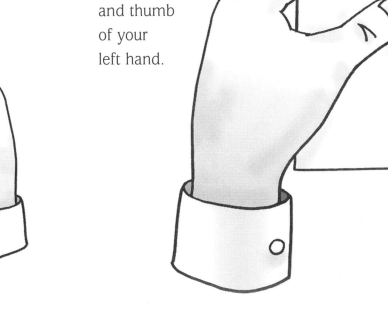

3. *"All I do is fold the paper ..."*

With your right hand, fold the bottom third of the paper up over the coin. Hold it with the first finger and thumb of your left hand.

" ... and fold the paper ... "

Fold back a third of the paper on the right side and hold it under your first finger.

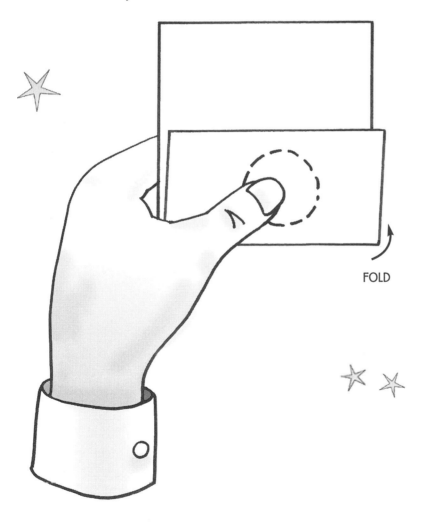

FOLD

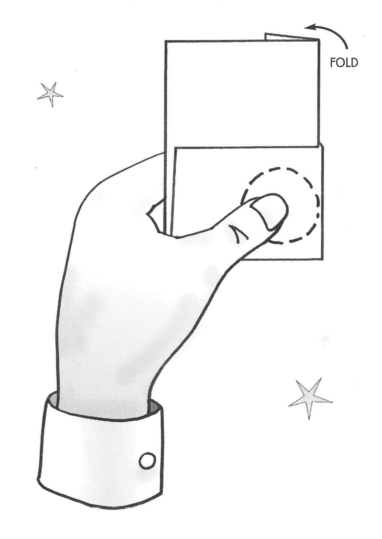

FOLD

Then fold back a third of the paper on the left side and hold it under your first finger.

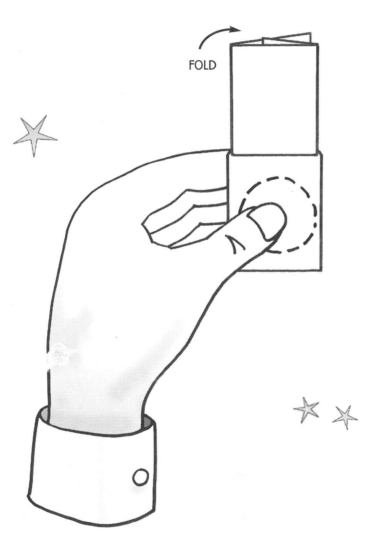

FOLD

"... *and fold the paper some more.*"

Fold down the top third of the paper and hold it under your first finger.

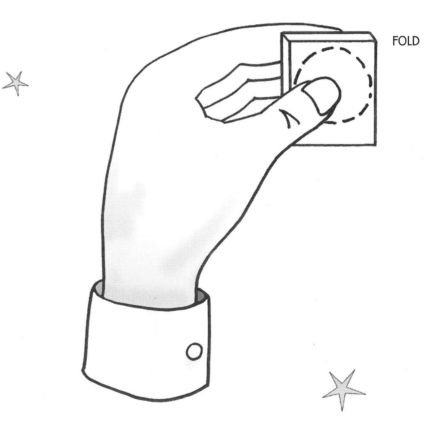

FOLD

4. *"And as you can see, the coin is still there."*

To convince the audience that the coin is wrapped in the paper, press the paper all around the coin to show its outline.

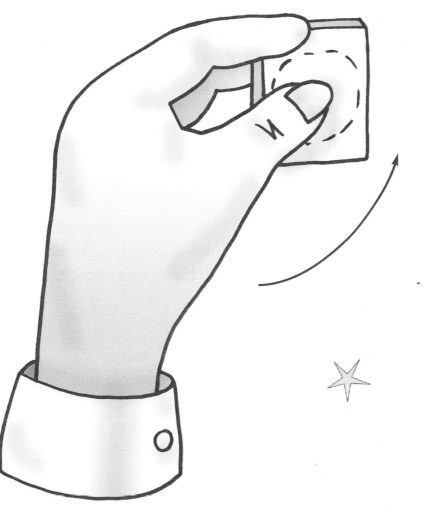

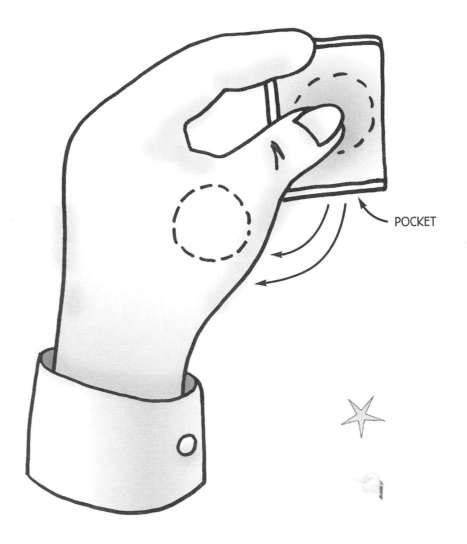

POCKET

As you are pressing the paper, turn it around so the open pocket is facing your palm. Let the coin secretly slide into your left palm.

5. *"But when I tear the paper in half … "*

Bring both hands together (still hiding the coin in your left palm) and tear the paper in half.

6. *"… the coin disappears!"*

Hand both pieces of paper to someone in the audience.

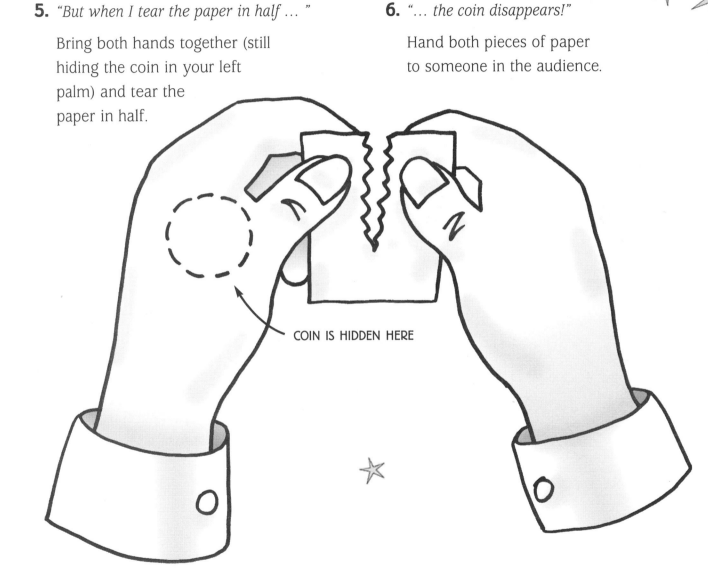

COIN IS HIDDEN HERE

Magical Mini-Routine

Perform the FOLD AWAY THE COIN TRICK, then reach up with your left hand (where you have the coin hidden) and perform the COIN FROM THE EAR TRICK (page 34), taking the coin from someone's ear or pocket or making it appear on his shoulder.

Tricks with Playing Cards

A magician always has a deck of cards handy. Here are some easy card tricks — I call them "self-working tricks" because you don't need to learn any special moves or fancy shuffles to perform them. If you follow the steps, they'll just happen. They're a great way to get comfortable handling cards and to develop confidence doing tricks with them. Once you become proficient with these tricks, you can go on to learn more advanced card-handling stunts and maneuvers.

Tonight at 8pm!!
Meet the
AMAZING
ADAM!
Come one, come all!

Before You Start ...

Fan the deck means spread the cards out like a fan:

Square the deck means stack the cards neatly with all the edges even.

Cut the deck means divide it into two sections:

FANNING THE DECK

CUTTING THE DECK

Double Reverse Card Trick

The magic: Two people pick cards, look at them, and put them back in the deck. The cards both magically turn over in the deck.

Prop: deck of cards

The trick:

1. With the cards facedown, fan the deck (page 46) slightly and ask two people to each pick a card. Have them look at their cards but they should not show them to you.

2. While the volunteers are looking at their cards, square the deck (page 46) and hold it behind your back. Turn the deck over so all the cards are facing up. Turn the top card over so it's facing down.

TURN DECK OVER SO CARDS FACEUP

TURN TOP CARD OVER SO FACING DOWN

3. Bring the deck out in front of you. All the cards are facing up except for the top card, which is facedown, so it will look to the audience as if the deck is facedown.

4. Take one card from one volunteer and place it facedown in the deck.

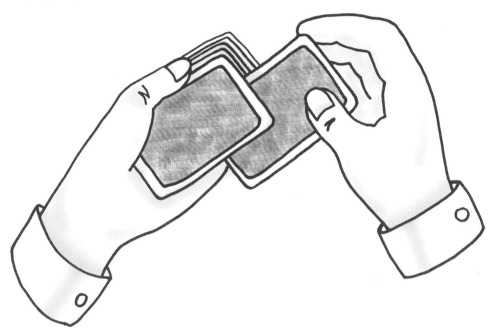

Take the other card and place it facedown in the deck. Don't spread the deck out and don't let the audience see the cards facing up.

5. Put the deck behind your back.

"Now I'll try to find the cards you picked."

Turn the top card over (faceup) and then turn the deck over so all the cards — *except* the two that you slipped back into the deck — are facedown.

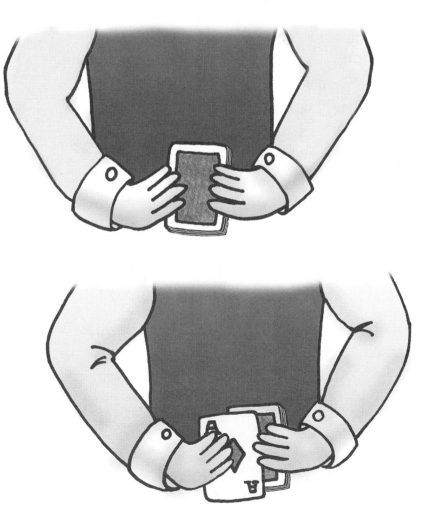

6. Bring the deck around in front of you. Spread out the cards either in your hands or on a table. The two selected cards will be faceup in the deck.

 **Don't overdo it!**
Only perform two or three card tricks at a time. People get tired of card tricks quickly. Making up a story to go with each trick or using a funny story to tie two or three tricks together might hold the audience's attention a little longer.

Countdown Card Trick

The magic: A volunteer picks a card from the deck, looks at it, and puts it back in the deck. You ask her to pick a number, you count down that many cards in the deck — and there is the card.

Props: deck of cards, table

The trick:

1. Holding the cards facedown, fan the deck (page 46), and ask a volunteer to pick a card from it.

2. *"Take a good look at your card and remember it."*

Square the top half of the deck (page 46) and have her put her card facedown on top of it.

3. Put the deck on the table and cut it (page 46).

4. Place the bottom half crosswise on top of the top half.

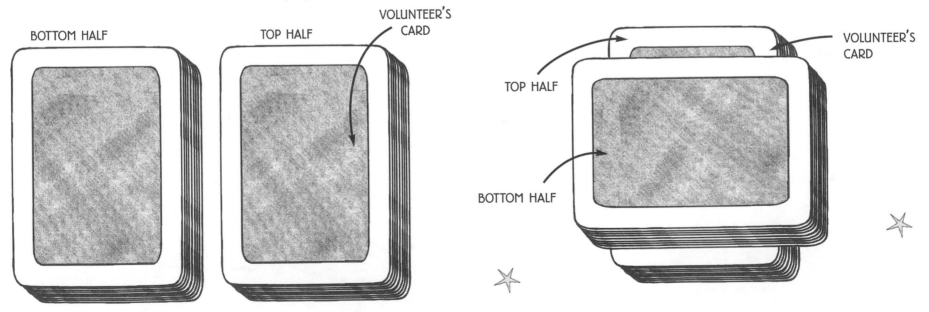

5. Now, here's the misdirection (page 10) for the audience so you can get the volunteer's card to end up where you want it:

"Now I'll ask you to help me find your card by picking a number. I'll count down that many cards and that's where your card will be."

While you're speaking, pick up the crosswise half of the deck and put it back on the table.

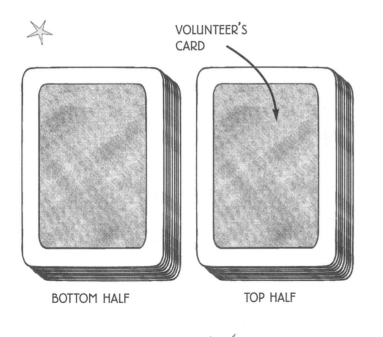

VOLUNTEER'S CARD

BOTTOM HALF   TOP HALF

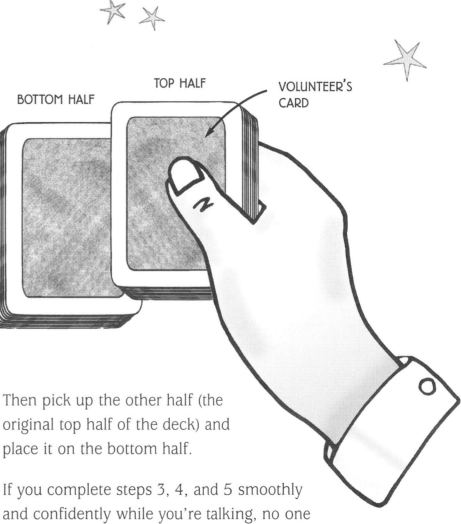

BOTTOM HALF   TOP HALF   VOLUNTEER'S CARD

Then pick up the other half (the original top half of the deck) and place it on the bottom half.

If you complete steps 3, 4, and 5 smoothly and confidently while you're talking, no one will realize that you have just placed the cards back in the same position you started with, with the volunteer's card on top.

FIFTEENTH CARD

6. Pick up the deck and square it. Ask the volunteer to pick a number from 10 to 25. Let's say she says 14. Deal out 14 cards facedown opposite the deck. Place the fifteenth card faceup on top.

7. *"Is that your card?"*

Of course she'll say "No" because her card is at the bottom of the pile.

8. *"That's funny. That's supposed to be your card."*

Pick up the pile of 15 cards that you just dealt out. Turn the top card back over and put those cards facedown on top of the deck. Now the card that she picked is 15 cards down from top of the deck.

9. *"I'll say the magic words, and this time you deal out the cards."*

Say your favorite magic word and hand the volunteer the deck of cards. Ask her to deal the top 14 cards while you count. Have her turn over the fifteenth card — it will be the one she picked at the beginning.

VOLUNTEER CARD IS NOW THE FIFTEENTH CARD IN THE DECK, AT THE BOTTOM OF THIS PILE

voila!

6 & 9 Card Trick

The magic: You place two cards in the middle of the deck and they move to the top of the deck.

Props: deck of cards, table

Preparation: Start the trick with the six of spades and the nine of clubs on top of the deck.

The trick:

1. *"I'll show you how to make two cards jump to the top of the deck. First you pick two cards."*

   Turn the deck faceup in your hands and sort through it to find the *six of clubs* and the *nine of spades* (not the cards you put on top of the deck).

2. Pull them from the deck and place them on the table so the audience can see them but don't name them.

3. *"Then you stick them into the middle of the deck."*

   Turn the deck facedown in your hands and slip the two cards into the middle of it. The *six of spades* and the *nine of clubs* on are still on top.

4. Square the deck (page 46) and place it on the table.

5. *"To get the cards to jump to the top of the deck, you have to knock on them a couple of times …"*

Knock on the top of the deck a few times.

6. *"… and both cards jump right to the top."*

Turn over the top two cards — the six of spades and the nine of clubs.

The Master Magician says …

Trick the eyes *and* the memory! *If you only **show** the six of clubs and the nine of spades at the beginning and don't name them, chances are no one will remember which one was the club and which one was the spade. Then when you turn over the six of **spades** and the nine of **clubs**, the audience will think they are the same cards.*

shazam!

Comedy Card Shuffle Trick

The magic: You show everyone what a great *card shark* (a person who is very skilled at handling cards as well as at card tricks and games) you are by throwing the cards from hand to hand as you shuffle.

Prop: comedy shuffle deck (page 57)

The trick:

1. *Does anyone know what these are?"*

Hold the stapled deck facedown in your left hand. The audience will answer.

2. *"Yes, they're cards, but they are trick cards. Some magicians can do a lot of tricks with them, but I can't."*

Place the deck on your left palm with your thumb and fingers on the outside of the deck.

come one, come all!
8pm friday
Leo the
Amazing
card shark!

3. With the thumb and fingers of your right hand, grasp the top of the deck lightly on the long edges. Now pull the deck up and down accordion style.

Don't pull too hard or you'll pull the deck apart. Practice in front of a mirror so it looks real.

4. *"Some magicians can even do it sideways."*

Pull the cards sideways with your right hand.

5. *"And even backward."*

Turn your back to them and do the shuffle.

bravo!

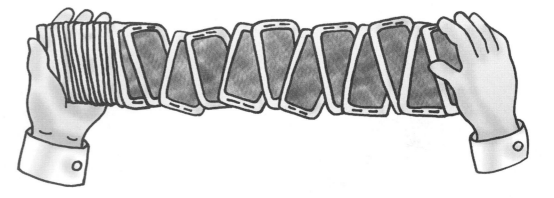

Making the Comedy Shuffle Deck

You need: old deck of cards (48 cards are plenty as long as they all have the same backs), stapler

To make the deck:

1. Place two cards with the same sides together, lining up the edges carefully. Staple them at one narrow end as shown.

STAPLE HERE

Do the same with the rest of the cards. You now have 24 sets of two cards stapled together.

2. Staple the unstapled end of one card in a set to the unstapled end of one card in another set.

NOW STAPLE HERE

ALREADY STAPLED

Continue stapling until you have all the sets stapled together accordion style.

Tricks with Rope

Magicians have been doing rope tricks for centuries. Even today, most professional magicians include at least one rope trick in their acts. And now you too can amaze your audience with what you can do using only a simple piece of rope!

Making the Magician's Rope

Magicians use a special magician's rope from a magic supply store (RESOURCES, pages 123 to 124). It's just white clothesline with the core removed. You can easily make your own by pulling the outer tube-like cover off cotton clothesline. (Be sure to check the label; many clotheslines are shiny synthetics that are too hard and stiff to use for tricks.)

You need: soft, white, cotton clothesline about $^3/8$" (1 cm) thick with a woven or braided outer cover; scissors

To make the magican's rope:

1. To practice pulling out the core, cut off a 6" (15 cm) piece of rope. Spread out the strands of the outer cover to expose about 1" (2.5 cm) of the inner core.

2. Hold the core with your right fingers and wrap your left hand around the outer cover. Pull the core up while you slide the outer cover down.

3. The outer cover will bunch up and the core will be hard to pull. Put your left hand down below the bunch and slide the cover down to straighten it out. Keep pulling and sliding until the core is pulled out. You'll be left with a soft, flexible tube.

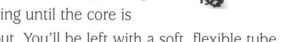

4. Once you've practiced with this short piece, you can core the 4' (1.5 m) piece of rope you need for the tricks in this chapter. If you are going to use the rope a lot, bind the ends so they won't fray. Just wrap them with a small piece of tape or dip them in glue and let them dry overnight.

Quick Knot Trick

The magic: You hold a rope between your two hands and with one simple motion a knot instantly appears.

Prop: 4' (1.5 m) piece of rope

The trick:

1. Hold your left hand with the palm facing you (as if you're reading something written on your palm). Place the rope under your left thumb with about 6" (15 cm) hanging behind your left hand. The long part of the rope hangs across your palm.

2. Hold your right hand with the palm facing you. Bring the other end of the rope up and over your right hand under your right thumb.

3. Pull about 8" (20 cm) of the rope under your right thumb to hang in front of your palm. The rope should now appear as shown.

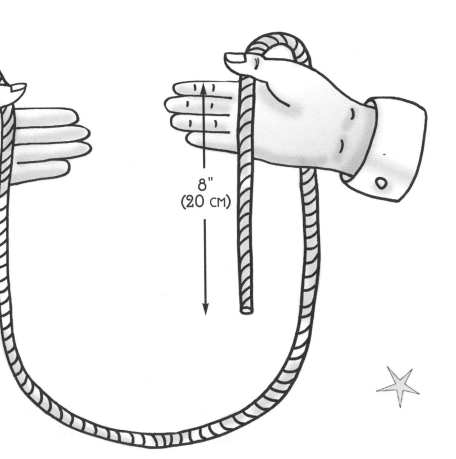

8"
(20 CM)

4. Hold both hands up to show the audience the rope hanging between them. Bring both hands together with the right fingers behind the left fingers.

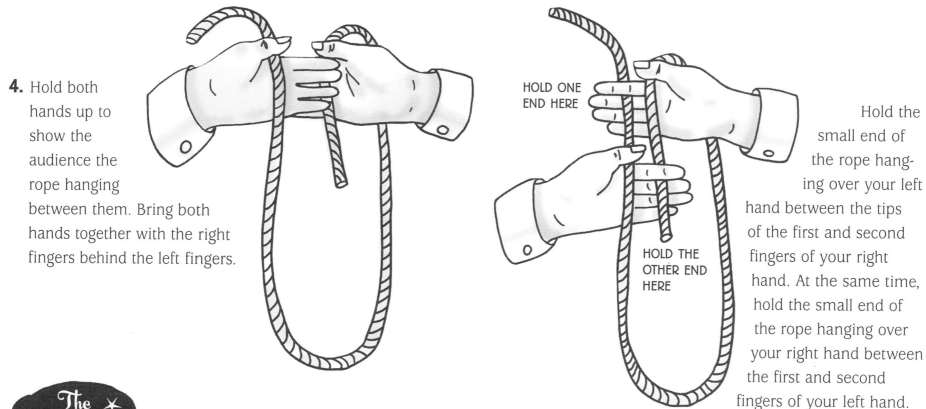

HOLD ONE END HERE

HOLD THE OTHER END HERE

Hold the small end of the rope hanging over your left hand between the tips of the first and second fingers of your right hand. At the same time, hold the small end of the rope hanging over your right hand between the first and second fingers of your left hand.

The *Master Magician* says ...

Hold them high! *When performing, hold the ropes at about shoulder height and out from your body so everyone can see them.*

5. Pull both hands straight out to the sides as you release your thumbs and an overhand knot "auto-magically" forms in the center of the rope. With practice, you'll be able to quickly touch your hands together and draw them apart, and a knot will appear.

Flick Knot Trick

The magic: You show the audience a piece of rope hanging over your hand. You shake your hand and a knot appears.

Prop: 4' (1.5 m) piece of rope

The trick:

1. Hold your right hand with the palm facing toward you. Hang the rope over your hand with half hanging in the front and the other half hanging in back.

2. With your left hand, take the piece hanging in back of your right hand, bring it up and in front of the other hanging section and place it between the first and second finger of your right hand so that about 2" (5 cm) of the rope is sticking up.

2" (5 CM)

3. Show the palm of your right hand to your audience. Hold on to the rope with your first and second finger and flick your right hand down.

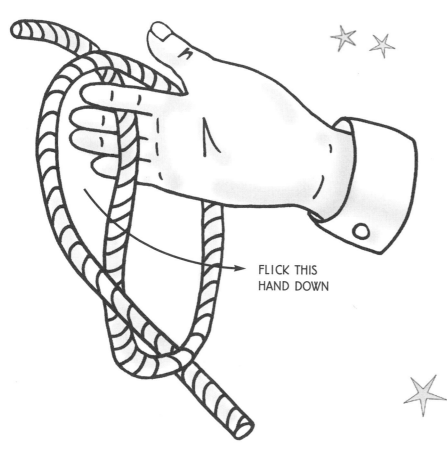

FLICK THIS
HAND DOWN

4. The loop will slide off your hand and make a knot in the rope.

The Master Magician says ...

No dirty ropes on stage! *Always use clean white rope when you're performing for an audience. Soiled or worn ropes are great for practice.*

Magical Mini-Routine

"There are many ways to tie a knot. You can just snap a knot out of rope like this."

Do the Flick Knot Trick (pages 62 to 63) with a 4' (1.5 m) piece of rope.

"Or you can hold the rope in both hands and tie a knot like this."

Do the Quick Knot Trick (pages 60 to 61).

"Or you can tie a regular knot like this."

Tie an overhand knot (left over right as shown).

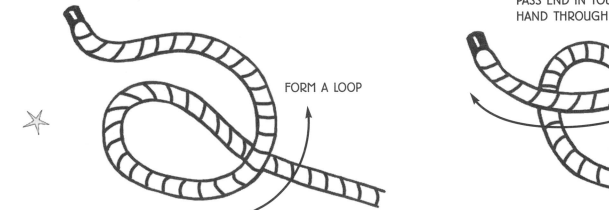

FORM A LOOP

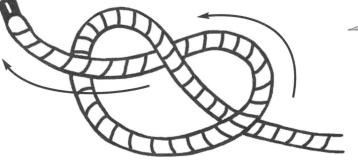

PASS END IN YOUR LEFT
HAND THROUGH LOOP

PULL

Vanishing Knot Trick

The magic: You tie a knot in a rope right in front of the audience. Snap your fingers and the knot disappears.

Prop: 4' (1.5 m) piece of rope

The trick:

1. Hold your left hand with the palm facing toward you. Place the rope between the first and second fingers of your left hand. About 6" (15 cm) of rope should be pointing up in front of your first finger. The rest of the rope is hanging down behind your second, third, and fourth fingers.

6"
(15 CM)

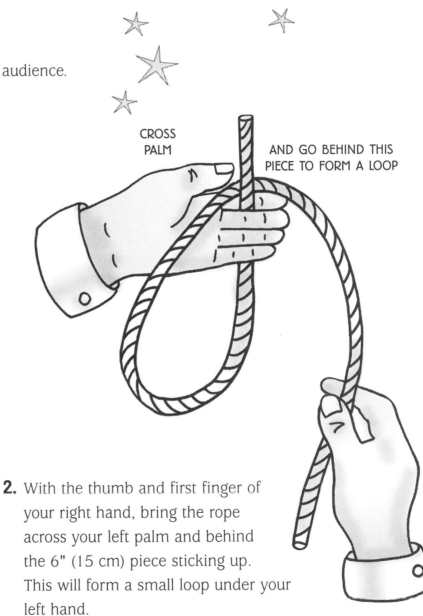

CROSS PALM

AND GO BEHIND THIS PIECE TO FORM A LOOP

2. With the thumb and first finger of your right hand, bring the rope across your left palm and behind the 6" (15 cm) piece sticking up. This will form a small loop under your left hand.

3. Pinch the crossed pieces of rope lightly between the thumb and first finger of your left hand.

4. Push the long end through the loop from behind so the rope comes out toward you.

5. Pull the short end of the rope up a little. Then pull the long end of the rope down a little. Alternate pulling up and down a little to make the false knot a little tighter.

PULL UP HERE

AND THEN DOWN HERE

6. Your thumb and first finger of your left hand are concealing the false knot. Pull the knot up tight to your thumb and first finger.

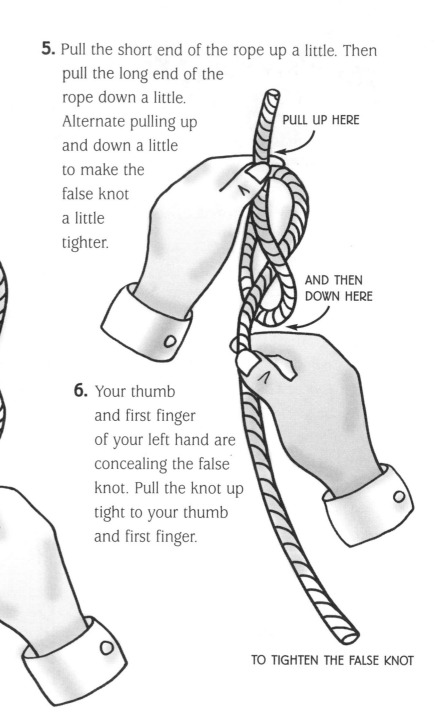

TO TIGHTEN THE FALSE KNOT

7. There are two ways to show that the knot is not a knot: Simply flick your left hand as you release the loop while you hold on to the upper end of the rope. The knot's gone!

Or, close your right hand over the knot in your left hand.

Hold the upper end of the rope with the thumb and first finger of your left hand.

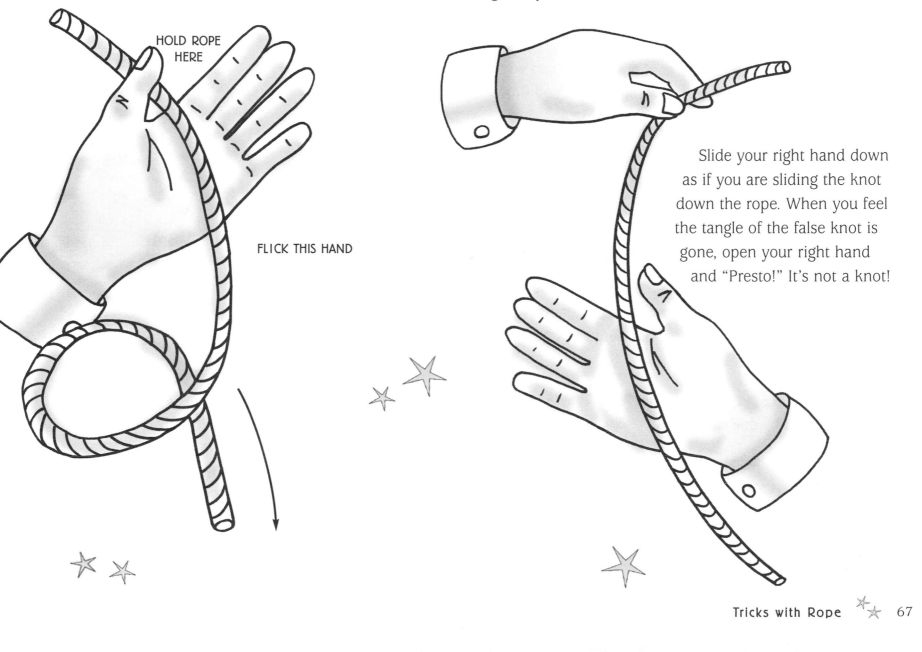

HOLD ROPE HERE

FLICK THIS HAND

Slide your right hand down as if you are sliding the knot down the rope. When you feel the tangle of the false knot is gone, open your right hand and "Presto!" It's not a knot!

Magical Mini-Routine

Props: audience volunteer, 4' (1.5 m) piece of rope, table

"I'm going to make a knot in this rope and you're going to hold it. Then I'm going to show you a good rope trick."

You make the vanishing knot through step 4 (VANISHING KNOT TRICK, page 65) and hand it to your volunteer as you turn away quickly to get something off the table. When you look back, your helper is holding a long rope.

"No, you're not supposed to untie it,"

you say as you take the rope back, make the vanishing knot again, hand it to her, and turn away. When you look back, your helper is holding a long rope again.

You take the rope back and hold it in your left hand by one end with your hand on your hip.

Explain that she wasn't supposed to take the knot out because you were going to do a trick. Tie either the quick knot (pages 60 to 61) or the flick knot (pages 62 to 63) –

"like this!"

"Not a Knot" Trick

The magic: You make a knot in a piece of rope, then you untie it. You make the knot again (the same way), but this time it's *not* a knot.

Prop: 4' (1.5 m) piece of rope

The trick:

1. Pinch each end of the rope between your thumb and the first finger of each hand. The second, third, and fourth fingers are curled back out of the way. About 4" (10 cm) of rope should be sticking up out of each hand.

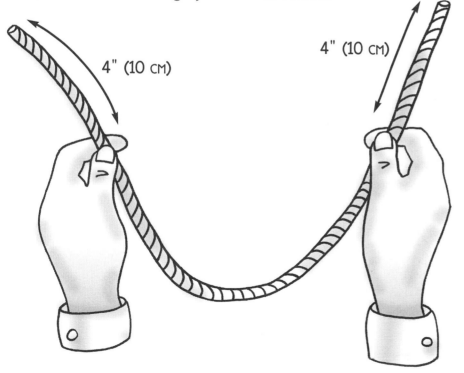

4" (10 CM)

4" (10 CM)

2. Bring your hands together and place the rope that's in your right hand in *front* of the rope in your left hand, pinching both ends between the thumb and first finger of your left hand. The two 4" (10 cm) ends are sticking up in a V and the rest of the rope is hanging down in a loop.

HOLD THE RIGHT-HAND ROPE IN FRONT OF THE LEFT-HAND ROPE

3. Grab the bottom of the loop with the thumb and first finger of your right hand. Pull the loop up and place it in the center of the V.

5. Pull your hands apart and a knot appears in the center of the rope.

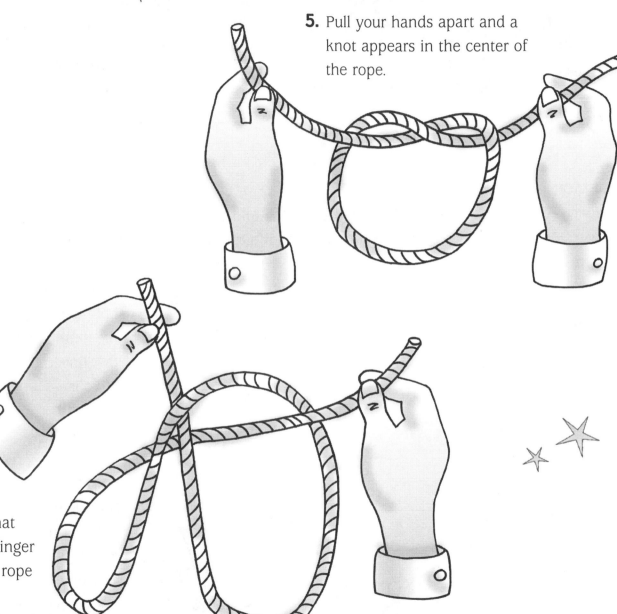

4. With the thumb and first finger of your right hand, hold the short end of the rope that is pointing to your right. As you pull that end to the right, slide the thumb and first finger of your left hand onto the short end of the rope that's pointing to the left.

6. Now, to make a knot not appear, do everything exactly the same way, except this time in step 2, place the rope in your right hand in *back* of the rope in your left hand (closer to the audience).

When you pull your hand apart, it's not a knot!

Once you get very good at doing these rope tricks without thinking about them, you can combine them in an old vaudeville routine (*vaudeville* is a type of stage entertainment with a variety of acts, including magic).

Didja' hear the one about the pig who walked into a restaurant?

Perform a series of rope tricks one after another while you tell short jokes. Many old-time vaudeville entertainers (including two very famous ones, W.C. Fields and Will Rogers) used this routine.

Tricks with Scarves

The magician waves her multicolored silk scarf over her assistant and *poof*, he disappears! The magician reaches up and magically draws colorful scarves out of thin air. He rolls up the scarves in his hands, says a magic word, and when he opens his hands, a dove appears!

Magicians perform many eye-catching tricks with colorful silk scarves. Here are some scarf tricks you can easily learn to do. OK, so maybe you won't make a dove appear, but you will be able to pass your magic wand right through a scarf without making a hole in it! For other tricks with scarves or handkerchiefs, see pages 72 to 82.

Poof!

✴ Magician's Silks ✴

For scarf tricks, magicians use silk scarves they call "silks." The fabric is thin so the scarves are easily concealed and when you use several at a time they aren't too bulky. The scarves are smooth and slippery so it's easy to manipulate them during a trick. And they come in lots of eye-catching colors! You can buy silks at a magic supply store (RESOURCES, pages 123 to 124). Or use handkerchiefs or bandannas. ✴

Three Scarves in the Air Trick

The magic: You roll three scarves into a ball and throw them up in the air. When they come down, they're knotted together.

Props: 3 scarves (MAGICIAN'S SILKS, page 72), handkerchiefs, or bandannas of different colors; small ¹/₂" (1 cm) rubber band close to your skin color; table

The trick:

1. *"Here I have a red scarf ..."*

Pick up the red scarf and the rubber band with your left hand, using the scarf to hide the rubber band.

2. Slide the rubber band onto the thumb and first two fingers of your right hand as you place a corner of the scarf between the thumb and first two fingers and the rubber band.

3. *"... a blue scarf ..."*

Pick up the second scarf and poke the corner next to the first one in between the thumb and first two fingers of your right hand and the rubber band.

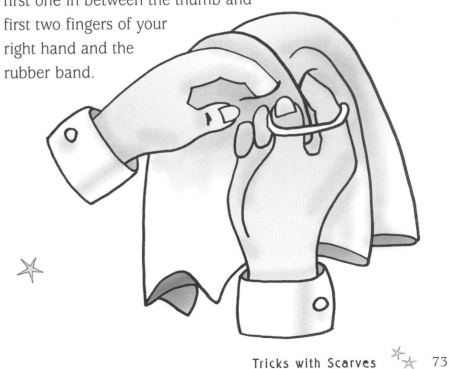

4. *"... and a white scarf."*

Do the same thing with the third scarf.

5. *"Now with an Abracadabra and a Hocus Pocus, they're all knotted together!"*

Roll the scarves into a ball as you slide the rubber band off your fingers onto the scarves.

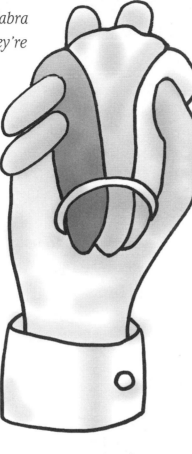

6. Throw the whole thing into the air. The scarves are all knotted together as you catch them.

The Master Magician says ...

But *this* scarf is the blue one! *To keep the audience from looking too closely at your hands and the rubber band, you can confuse the colors of the scarves. When you hold up the red one, say it's white and everyone will correct you. You complain that it can't be red because this one is red (holding up the blue one), and they'll tell you it's blue. No, you say, that one can't be blue because ... well, you get the idea!*

Right Through the Scarf Trick

The magic: You make a pencil, magic wand, or any long, straight object go straight through a scarf without making a hole in it.

Props: scarf (Magician's Silks, page 72), handkerchief, or bandanna; pencil or magic wand; table

The trick:

1. *"All magicians use secret compartments and trapdoors to do their tricks."*

With the back of your left hand facing the audience, make a circle with the thumb and first finger.

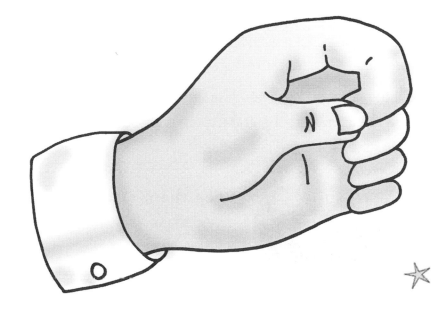

2. Drape the scarf over your left hand. Push the first finger of your right hand down into the scarf and the circle of your left hand to make a small well.

3. *"Sometimes magicians have to make their own secret compartments and trapdoors."*

Use the pencil to poke the scarf into the well. As you poke, open your left hand slightly to form a C.

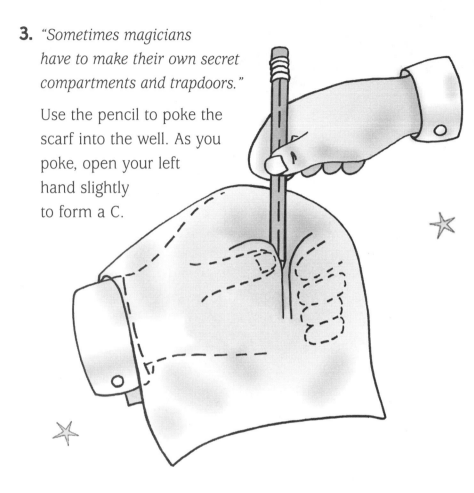

4. As you poke the pencil into the scarf, the pencil is forming a channel between your thumb and fingers. Close your left hand, holding both the pencil and the scarf.

5. Reach underneath the scarf with your right hand and slowly pull the pencil down and out. (Make sure you reach *underneath* the scarf to pull out the pencil so that it looks to the audience as if you're pulling the pencil *through* the scarf. *Don't* reach from the side.)

6. *"Then we have to quickly get rid of all the secret compartments and trapdoors before we finish the trick."*

Pull the scarf off your left hand and shake it. Hold it up to show it has no secret compartments, trapdoors, or holes.

Keep them clean! *Use only clean, wrinkle-free scarves. Shabby-looking props spoil a performance.*

Scarf Through the Glass Trick

The magic: You stuff a scarf into a glass, cover the glass with another scarf, and then slowly pull the first scarf through the bottom of the glass.

Props: small straight-sided drinking glass; 2 different-colored scarves (MAGICIAN'S SILKS, page 72), handkerchiefs, or bandannas, one large enough to stay inside the glass when you turn it upside down; rubber band; table

The trick:

1. *"Sometimes drinking glasses have secret compartments and trapdoors."*

   With the thumb and first two fingers of your right hand, hold up the drinking glass by the bottom. The mouth of the glass should be facing up.

2. Pick up one scarf with your left hand and show it to the audience. Stuff the scarf into the glass. Pick up the second scarf with your left hand and show it to the audience.

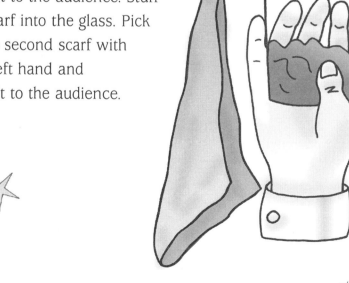

3. Bring the scarf up in front of the glass so it hides the glass from the audience's view. As you begin to cover the glass, allow it to turn upside down between the thumb and first two fingers of your right hand. Drape the scarf over the glass.

4. *"It's not always easy to find the secret compartments and trapdoors because sometimes they're even hidden from the magician."*

Under the scarf, switch the glass (still upside down) to your left hand and remove your right hand. Pick up the rubber band with your right hand and put it around the scarf and glass.

5. *"But if you know where to look, it's easy."*

Reach up underneath the scarf with your right hand and slowly pull the other scarf out of the glass. Show it to the audience and put it on the table.

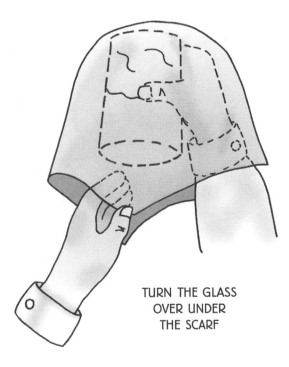

TURN THE GLASS
OVER UNDER
THE SCARF

PULL OUT SCARF WITH YOUR RIGHT HAND

6. *"Then you have to close the secret compartments and trapdoors and end the trick."*

Reach back underneath the scarf with your right hand and switch the glass to your thumb and first two fingers of that hand.

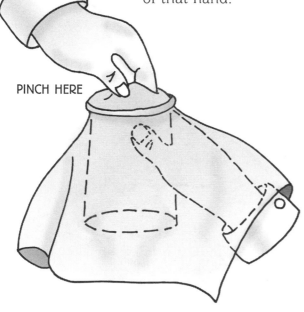

PINCH HERE

Bring your left hand out and use it to pinch the scarf with the thumb and first two fingers in the middle on top of the glass.

7. Pull up the scarf a little with your left hand so that the rubber band slides off the glass. Don't pull it up quickly. Give yourself time to swing the glass back to its original position with the mouth facing up. As soon as the glass is upright, pull off the handkerchief.

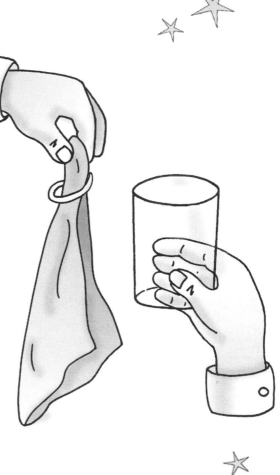

Hypnotized Scarf Trick

The magic: You hypnotize a scarf so that it obeys your commands.

Props: scarf (MAGICIAN'S SILKS, page 72), handkerchief, or bandanna; magic wand (optional)

The trick:

1. *"Have you ever watched a magician hypnotize someone? Did you know it's easy to hypnotize a scarf as well?"*

   Pinch the center of the scarf with your right hand.

2. Place the scarf against your left palm and close your fingers lightly around the scarf.

3. Pull the scarf up about 5" or 6" (12.5 to 15 cm) above your left hand. The scarf should now be standing straight up.

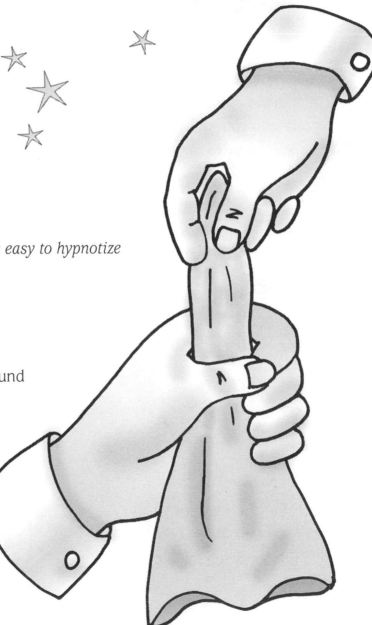

4. *"Hocus Pocus, you are now under my command."*

Secretly raise your left thumb behind the scarf.

Do some hypnotizing moves over the scarf with your right hand or your wand.

5. Motion with your right hand to the front and at the same time move the thumb of your left hand up the scarf. The scarf will move to the front.

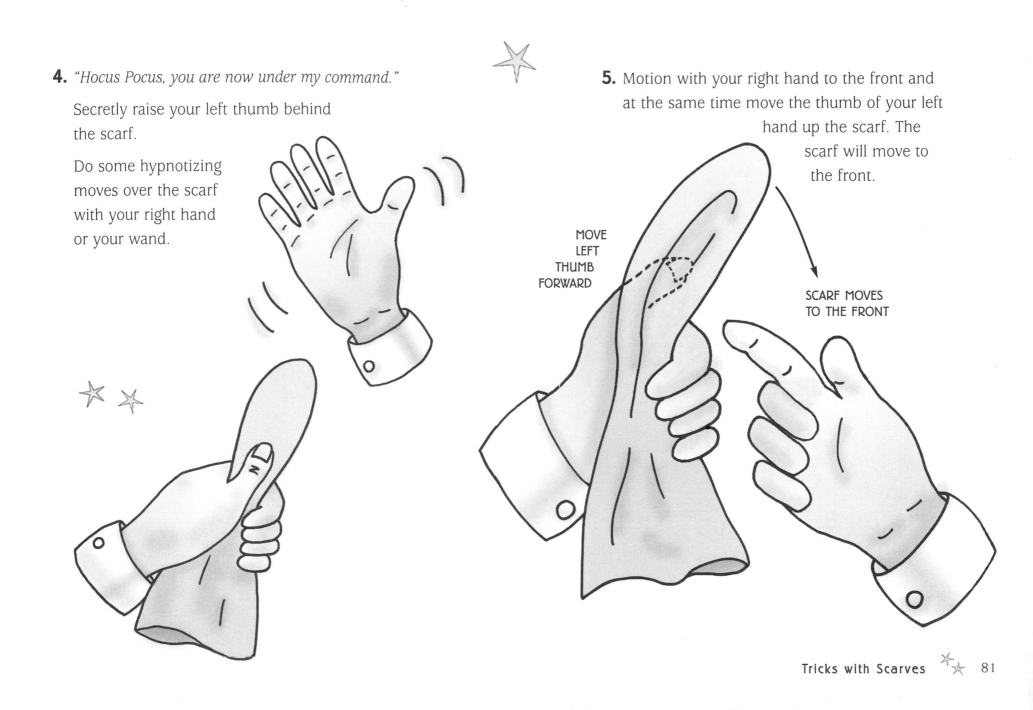

MOVE
LEFT
THUMB
FORWARD

SCARF MOVES
TO THE FRONT

6. Motion with your right hand to the back and at the same time move the thumb of your left hand down the scarf. The scarf will move to the back. Repeat a couple of times.

7. *"Play dead."*

Release your thumb and the scarf will fall over your hand.

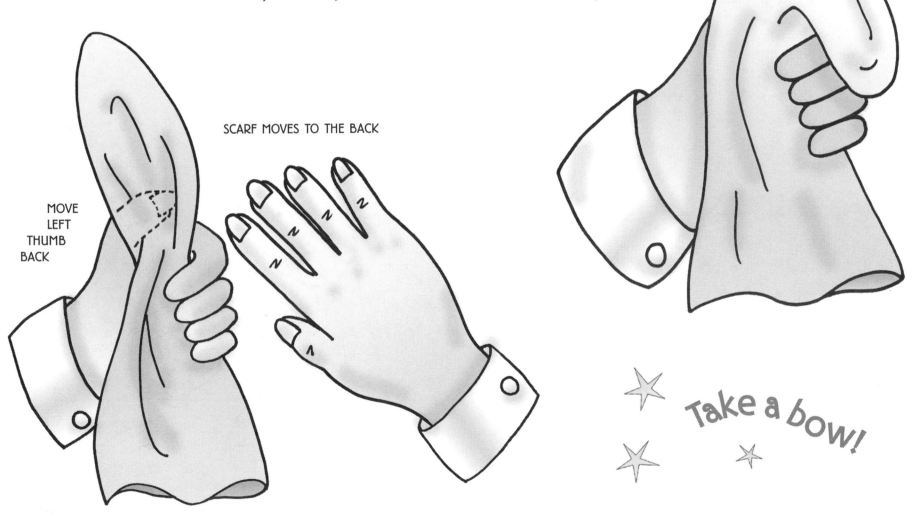

SCARF MOVES TO THE BACK

MOVE LEFT THUMB BACK

Take a bow!

Tricks with Eating Utensils

Just like everybody else, we magicians aren't supposed to play with our food. But we can play with our utensils. These tricks are called table tricks because you do them at a table — either at home, in a restaurant, or in the school cafeteria. It's a great way to keep your family entertained while you're waiting for your meal to come in a restaurant.

You can use different utensils than the ones I chose. You also can do the same tricks with magic wands, rulers, pencils, or pens.

Allakazam, Allakazake, Please bring me a forkful of that chocolate cake!

Spoon Switcheroo Trick

The magic: Sitting at a table, you roll a spoon up into a napkin. When you unroll it, it has turned into a fork.

Props: chair, table, fork, cloth napkin, spoon

Preparation: Sit at the table. Place the fork on the table while laying a napkin down. If you don't call too much attention to yourself, you can probably lay the fork down and put the napkin over it before anyone realizes that you're starting to do a trick. Place the napkin so it forms a diamond with the lowest point facing you and the highest point facing away from you.

FORK IS UNDER HERE

KEEP THE NAPKIN LOOSE SO IT HIDES THE FORK UNDERNEATH

The trick:

1. *"You know, sometimes at a restaurant they give you a spoon and what you really need is a fork."*

   Place the spoon on the napkin so it is nestled on top of the fork hidden underneath.

2. *"But if you know a little magic …"*

With the thumb, first, and second fingers of both hands, start to roll up both the fork and the spoon in the napkin. Slide the napkin under the fork with your thumbs and roll the napkin, fork, and spoon away from you.

3. Keep rolling until the bottom point of the napkin rolls up to become the top point and the other point is facing you.

4. *"… you can always help yourself … "*

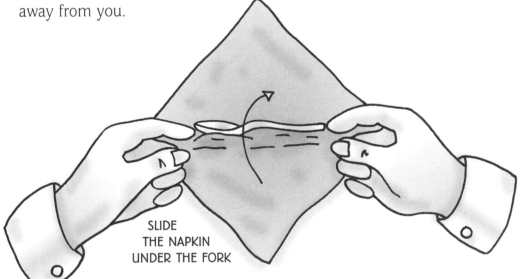

SLIDE
THE NAPKIN
UNDER THE FORK

BOTTOM POINT

Hold the new top point with the thumb and first finger of your right hand. Hold the point facing toward you with the thumb and first finger of your left hand.

The Master Magician says …

Perform more "switcheroos"! *You can do this trick with magic wands, rulers, pencils, or pens. You could change a big wand into a small one, a red pencil to a yellow one, a pen into a pencil, a ruler into a magic wand … you get the idea.*

5. Pull the two corners in opposite directions. As you do, slide the napkin back toward you and the edge of the table.

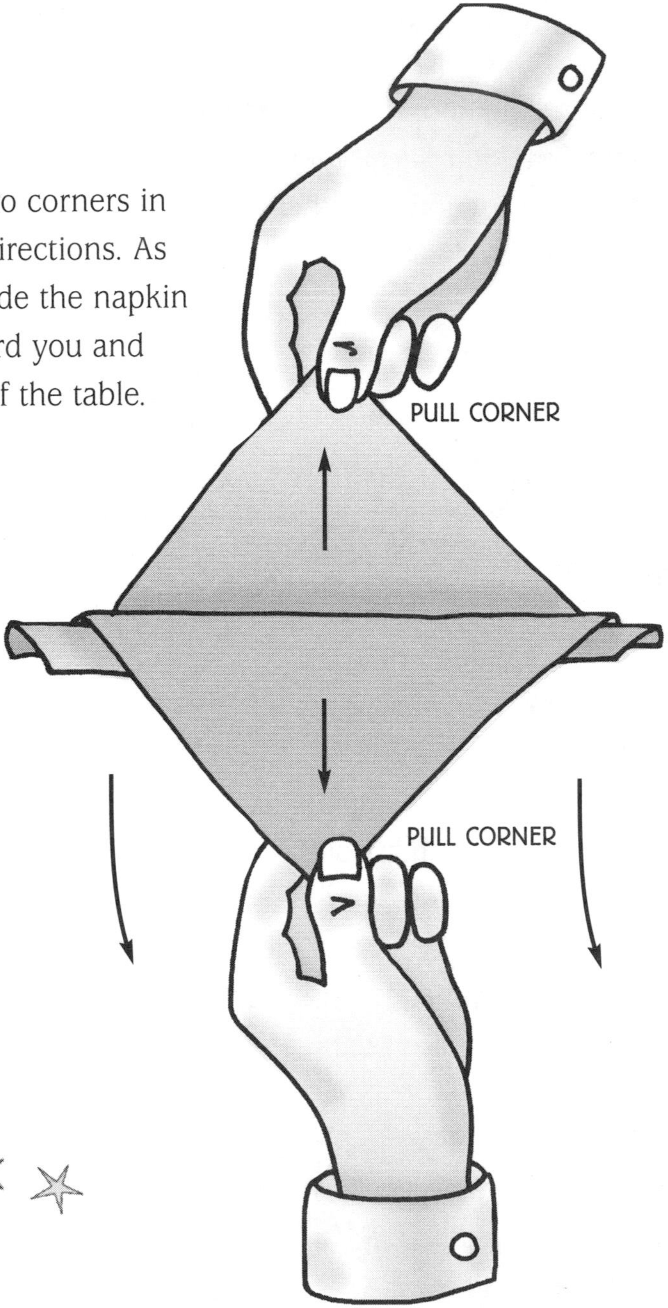

PULL CORNER

PULL CORNER

6. *"... and change the spoon into the fork you need. Ta-da!"*

The napkin will unroll flat onto the table with the fork on top and the spoon will fall into your lap.

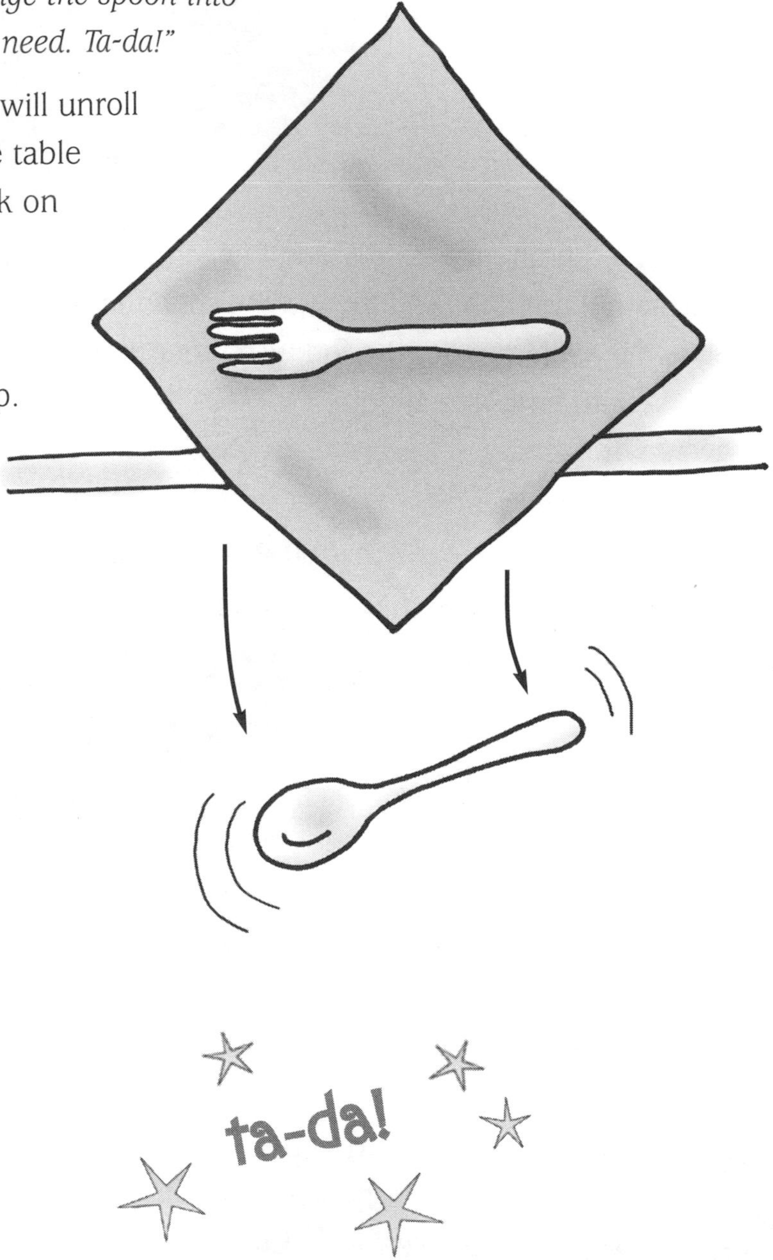

ta-da!

Sticky Fingers Trick

The magic: You tell everyone that you're going to make a fork stick to your hand by magic. Your first attempt fails but the second time, with great concentration, you make it stay!

Props: table, chair, fork

The trick:

1. *"Sometimes I can make an ordinary fork hang from my hand."*

Sit at the table and show the audience the fork.

"It just takes great concentration."

2. Place your left elbow on the table in front of you and hold your left hand up with the palm facing toward you. Place the fork in your left hand with the prongs pointing up. Close your left hand around the fork.

3. *"I'll hold my wrist to steady it."*

Hold your left wrist with your right hand.

Open your left hand slowly — the fork falls onto the table.

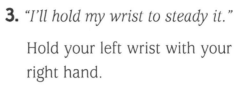

4. *"I guess I didn't concentrate hard enough. Let's try it again."*

Repeat the actions in steps 2 and 3 (page 87), only this time when you hold your left wrist with your right hand, you secretly extend your first finger out to hold the fork in place.

SECRETLY HOLD THE FORK
WITH YOUR FIRST FINGER

encore! encore!

5. *"Concentrate, concentrate."*

Slowly open your left hand. To the audience, it looks as if the fork is hanging magically from your hand.

WHAT THE AUDIENCE SEES

Fork Through a Glass Trick

The magic: You try to push a fork through the bottom of a glass. It clinks on the bottom of the glass. You try again but it still clinks. On the third try, it goes right through the glass.

Props: glass, fork

The trick:

1. *"Have you ever seen a utensil magically go through the bottom of a glass?"*

Hold a glass upside down in your left hand with your palm facing toward you. Hold the fork in your right hand with the prongs pointing up.

2. Slide the fork up the inside of glass until the prongs hit the bottom of the glass and make a noise. Pull the fork out and look at it.

"I wonder how they do that?"

3. Push the fork back into the glass and hit the bottom of the glass again. Pull the fork out and look at it.

"It looks so easy when a magician does it."

4. This time slide the fork up the outside until it pokes out above the top.

To the audience it looks as if the fork went through the bottom of the glass.

"Hey! I did it. I guess I just found the right spot.

Take a bow!

Magical Mini-Routine

Start by changing the spoon into a fork (SPOON SWITCHEROO TRICK, page 84) and then use the fork in two more tricks (STICKY FINGERS TRICK, page 87, and FORK THROUGH A GLASS TRICK, page 89).

Where's all the silverware?!?

Tricks with Props

Here I'll show you how to create a few fun props so you can make things (even a person!) disappear right in front of the audience's eyes or appear where people aren't expecting them (you read a sock sale ad in the newspaper and out pop the socks!). Unlike the other props in this book, such as the stapled cards in COMEDY CARD SHUFFLE TRICK (page 55), which are for that specific trick only, these props can be used in a variety of ways in your show. Whether you want to stump people with items that come and go or make them laugh as you do your silly shopping, you'll find they're perfect when you need to create an effect or when you want to clown around and tell a few jokes.

Disappearing Item Trick

The magic: You place a small item in a bag and say the magic word, and the item disappears.

Props: paper change bag (page 94); small or flat item, such as a playing card, dollar bill, or small handkerchief (MAGICIAN'S SILKS, page 72); table; magic wand

The trick:

1. Place the bag and the item to disappear on the table. Hold the bag in your left hand with your first finger in the secret compartment (to keep it open) and the other three fingers in the bag. Your thumb is on the outside of the bag.

2. Keep the bag upright so the audience can't see into it. Pick up the item to disappear with your right hand and place it in the secret compartment.

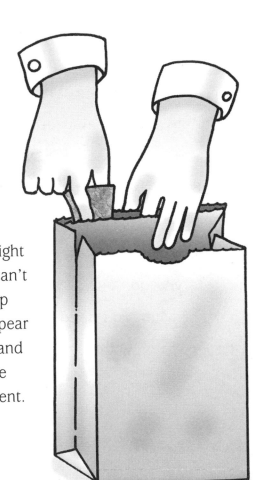

3. Take your left hand out of the bag and pick up your magic wand. Transfer the wand to your right hand and put your left hand back in the bag to pick it up. Put all four fingers of your left hand inside the bag to hold the secret compartment closed and place your thumb on the outside of the bag.

4. Wave your magic wand over the bag and say some magic words. Put down the wand and grab the front top edge of the bag with your right hand.

GRAB THE BAG HERE

5. Hold the bag securely with your left hand and pull down quickly with your right hand to tear open the bag and dramatically show that it is empty.

After everyone has seen the empty bag, discard it so they don't see the secret compartment.

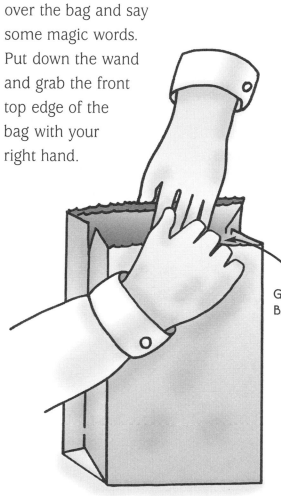

Making the Paper Change Bag

The change bag is a basic magician's prop. It looks like an ordinary lunch bag but it has a secret compartment so you can make things disappear or change one item into another, like one playing card into another or a handkerchief into a card, for example. Magic shops sell many different kinds, but you can easily make your own from a paper bag.

You need: 2 brown lunch bags, scissors, glue

To make the bag:

1. Open one bag and cut it in half as shown. You only need one half (but save the other one to make another change bag later).

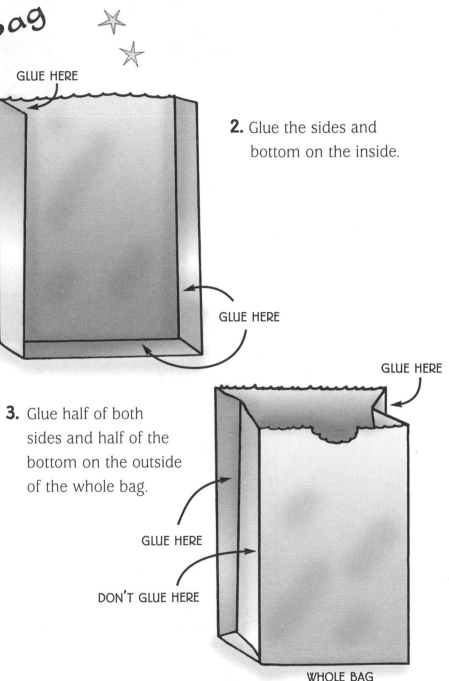

GLUE HERE

2. Glue the sides and bottom on the inside.

GLUE HERE

GLUE HERE

3. Glue half of both sides and half of the bottom on the outside of the whole bag.

GLUE HERE

DON'T GLUE HERE

WHOLE BAG

4. Finally, tear two 1" (2.5 cm) slits in the sides of the bag just in front of the glued-on pieces. These slits will make it easier to tear the bag at the end of the trick.

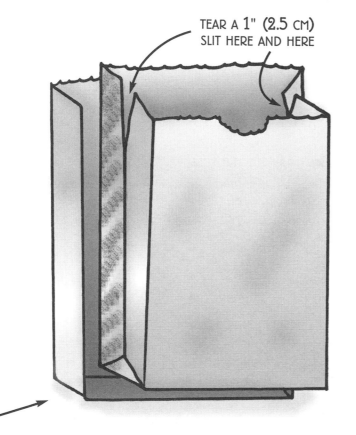

TEAR A 1" (2.5 CM) SLIT HERE AND HERE

5. Place the half bag over the whole bag as shown so the glued edges meet. Press down and smooth out all the glued sides. Remove any excess glue along the edges. The unglued back side forms the secret compartment.

Want to Hide Something Larger?

To make a larger change bag, use two large paper grocery bags. Make a secret compartment that same way you did with the lunch bags (MAKING THE PAPER CHANGE BAG, page 94). Now you can use bigger and bulkier props. Start by hiding a stuffed animal (or an action figure or your favorite doll) in the full bag. Make a drawing of the item in front of your audience or tear a picture of it out of a magazine. Slip the picture into the secret compartment, say the magic words, and tear open the bag. Out jumps the animal!

The Master Magician says ... **Presto change-o! Now it's yellow!** *You can use the change bag to change the color of an item. Let's say you want to change a red handkerchief to a yellow one. Before you start the trick, put the yellow handkerchief in the front bag. Show the red handkerchief and slip it into the secret compartment. Tear the bag open to reveal ... a yellow handkerchief!*

Magic Box Trick

The magic: You display a decorated box with no top or bottom and show the audience that it's empty. You display a decorated tube with no top or bottom and show that it is also empty. You place the tube inside the box, say a few magic words, and pull out a string of brightly colored scarves or handkerchiefs. (For more scarf tricks, see pages 72 to 82.)

Props: table; magic box and tubes (page 98); small tray; silk scarves or handkerchiefs (MAGICIAN'S SILKS, page 72), tied end to end to form a streamer; magic wand

Preparation: Slide the larger decorated tube over the smaller black tube and place it on the tray. Stuff the streamer into the smaller tube. Place the box over the tubes with the cutout window facing the audience.

The trick:

1. Lift the box off the tubes and show it to the audience. *Don't* say "I have here an empty box," just twirl it around, look through it — anything to demonstrate that it's empty. Put the box back over the tubes.

2. Lift out the decorated tube without moving the smaller black tube. When the audience looks through the window of the square, they'll see "black" and they'll think the square is empty.

Flash the decorated tube around, look through it, poke your magic wand through it — in other words, prove that it too is empty.

3. Place the decorated tube inside the box, sliding it back over the black tube.

4. Say the magic words, wave your wand, and pull out the string of silks or handkerchiefs out of the tube.

Making the Magic Box and Tubes

You need: scissors, poster board, ruler, black tempera paint, paintbrush, brightly colored adhesive-backed paper or markers, glue

To make the box and tubes:

1. Measure and cut the poster board into three rectangles as shown.

2. Paint or decorate as shown. Let dry.

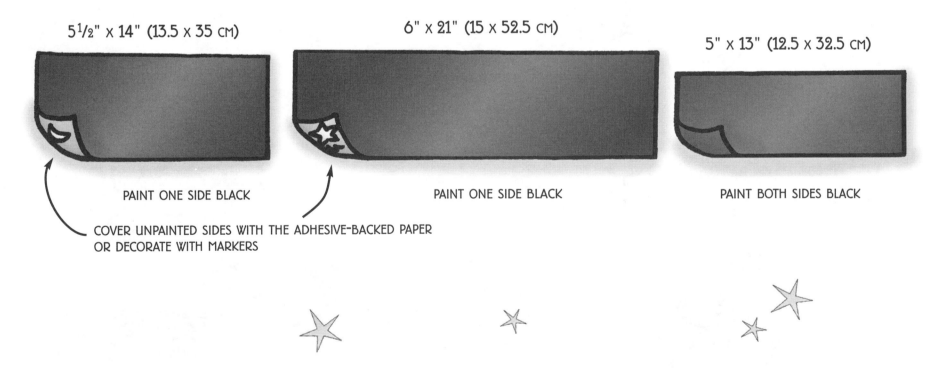

5¹/₂" x 14" (13.5 x 35 CM)

6" x 21" (15 x 52.5 CM)

5" x 13" (12.5 x 32.5 CM)

PAINT ONE SIDE BLACK

PAINT ONE SIDE BLACK

PAINT BOTH SIDES BLACK

COVER UNPAINTED SIDES WITH THE ADHESIVE-BACKED PAPER
OR DECORATE WITH MARKERS

3. Roll the black 5" x 13" (12.5 x 32.5 cm) piece into a short tube, overlapping the edges 1" (2.5 cm); glue the overlap. Roll the 5$\frac{1}{2}$" X 14" (13.5 x 35 cm) piece into a short tube, with the brightly colored side facing out, and glue the 1" (2.5 cm) overlap.

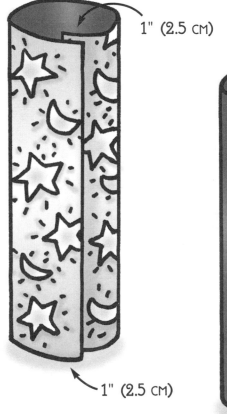

1" (2.5 CM)

1" (2.5 CM)

4. Place the 6" x 21" (15 x 52.5 cm) piece, brightly colored side down, on a table. Make four folds as shown, always folding in the same direction.

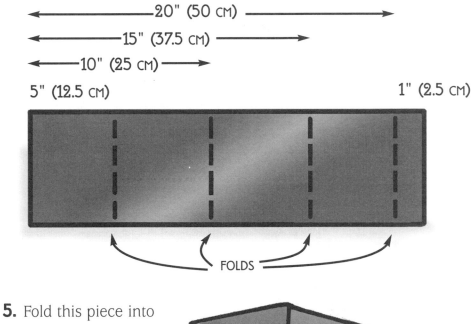

20" (50 CM)

15" (37.5 CM)

10" (25 CM)

5" (12.5 CM)

1" (2.5 CM)

FOLDS

5. Fold this piece into a box (with no top or bottom) with the decorated side facing out. Cut a design into one of the 5" x 6" (12.5 x 15 cm) sides. Glue the overlap.

OVERLAP THE 1" (2.5 CM) FLAP AND GLUE IT DOWN

CUTOUT DESIGN

Paper Cone Trick

The magic: You show the audience both sides of a newspaper, then you roll it up into a cone. You snap your fingers, say a magic word, reach into the cone, and pull out a bunch of brightly colored scarves or ribbons. (For more scarf tricks, see pages 72 to 82.)

Props: trick newspaper (page 102); small, colorful handkerchiefs, bandannas, scarves (MAGICIAN'S SILKS, page 72), or ribbons, tied end to end

Preparation: Fill the secret pocket with the handkerchiefs, scarves, or ribbons.

The trick:

1. *"Here's today's newspaper."*

Hold the trick newspaper by the top edges and show the audience both sides.

2. Turn it sideways and roll it into a cone by folding the edge with the secret pocket full of handkerchiefs toward the center of the newspaper as shown. The pocket will now be on the inside of the cone, facing up.

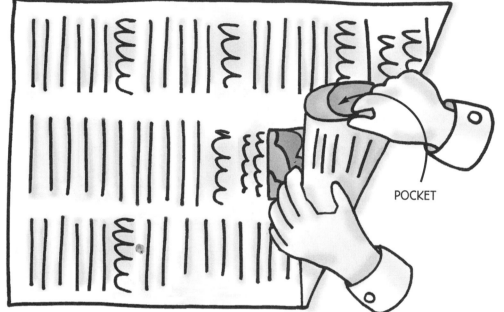

POCKET

FOLD IS ALONG THE BOTTOM

3. *"Abraca blanky. Swanky panky. Make a bunch of little hankies."*

Pull out the handkerchiefs.

Making the Trick Newspaper

You need: full-size double sheet of newspaper, unfolded; glue

To make the newspaper:

1. Glue one side of the unfolded sheet as shown.

2. Fold the sheet over and press into place; let dry.

POCKET IS HERE

The Master Magician says ...

Disappearing handkerchief. *You can also reverse this trick to make a handkerchief disappear. Roll up the trick newspaper. Place a handkerchief into the secret pocket. Unroll the cone and the handkerchief has disappeared.*

Magic Shopping Trick

The magic: You read newspaper ads aloud to the audience — and the ads come to life! For example, when you read about a sale on gloves, you immediately show off a pair of gloves. You read an ad for socks — and the socks are right there in your hand.

Prop: magic advertising section (page 105)

The trick:

1. *"It is so much easier shopping with magic than shopping at the mall."*

   Display the trick sheet of newspaper front and back.

2. *"Here's an ad for a Sweet & Sickening Candy Bar, guaranteed to rot your teeth. Wow! And it has a five-day daily requirement of sugar, PLUS it's sticky and gooey and will make a mess anywhere you leave it."*

3. Holding the newspaper in your left hand, snap the first finger of your right hand against the square with the candy bar and the paper will split.

   Pull the candy bar out and display it. Then make a show of putting it down carefully, as if it's sticky.

presto!

4. *"Have you been wearing the same stinky, smelly socks all week? Don't you think it's time for a new pair?"*

You snap the newspaper again and show off a really ugly sock.

5. *"Do you have a hard time picking up things with gloves on? What you need are fingerless gloves. Of course, they don't keep your hands warm but you can pick up a dime."*

Snap and show off the fingerless glove.

6. *"Does your mom want you to brush your teeth twice a day and you really don't want to?"*

You snap and show a toothbrush with no bristles.

"Now you can look like you're brushing even when you're not."

You fake brushing your teeth.

7. *"So if you're tired of running around the malls looking for things, just let your fingers do the walking magically through your local newspaper."*

You fold up the newspaper and put it away.

Making the Magic Advertising Section

You need: full-size double sheet of newspaper, glue, four small lightweight items such as a glove, a sock, a toothbrush, and an empty candy wrapper

To make the magic section:

1. Tear the newspaper down the center fold to make two sheets.

2. Place one sheet on a flat surface and glue the top, bottom, sides, and four squares as shown. Place an item in each square. To make it funny, you can use a glove with the fingers cut off, a really ugly sock, a tooth-brush with dirty or cut-off bristles, and a candy bar wrapper stuffed with tissue paper to make it look full.

Place the other sheet of paper over the glued sheet and press it into place around the edges and around the squares; let dry.

Use your imagination! *You can use any items you want as long as they are small, lightweight, and not too bulky. And of course you can also make up your own silly jokes instead of using mine!*

Disappearing Person Trick

The magic: Your assistant steps into a large cardboard box and you close it up. You say the magic words, open the box, and tip it forward. Your assistant has disappeared.

Props: big magic box (page 108), assistant

Preparation: Place the box on the floor as shown; the side with the handle should be facing the audience.

The trick:

1. Open the box and have your assistant step into it and sit down. Your assistant should crouch down and sit very still, holding the handle.

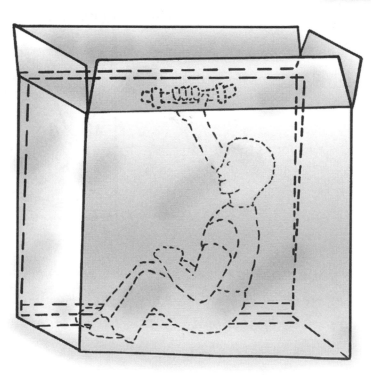

2. Close the flaps and say the magic words. Tilt the box forward, leaving your assistant sitting on the cardboard flap behind the box. As you tip the box, he holds the handle to pull the false bottom up into place.

3. When the box is completely tipped on its side, open the flaps to show that your assistant has vanished.

4. Close the flaps. Tilt the box back to its upright position. As you tip it, your assistant pushes the false bottom back down and then sits quietly without moving as the box comes back down around him.

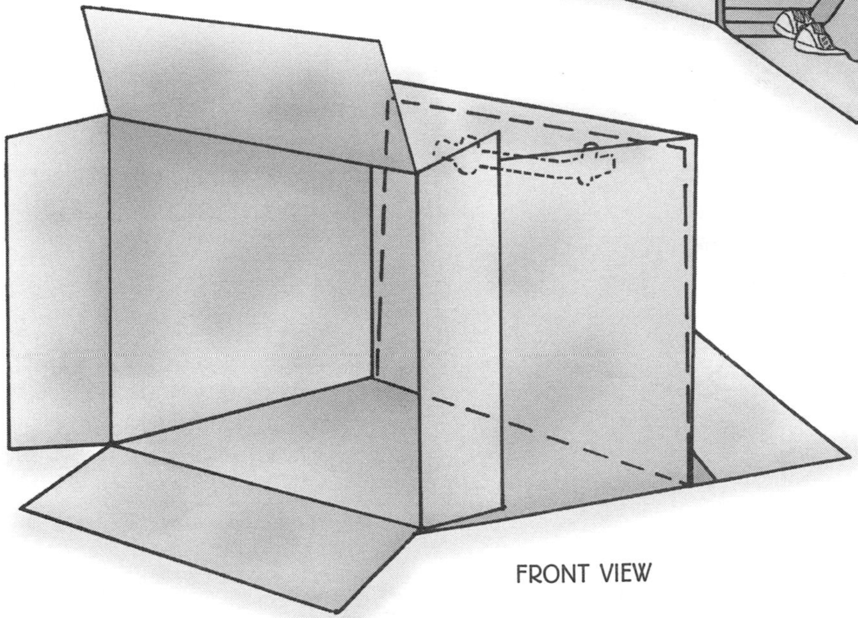

5. Open the flaps and your assistant steps out of the box.

BACK VIEW

FRONT VIEW

shazam!

Making the Big Magic Box

You need: scissors or utility knife (for use with grown-up help), 2 cardboard boxes both big enough to hide your assistant when sitting inside, ruler, masking tape, black tempera paint, paintbrush

To make the box:

1. Cut the bottom flaps off of one box, leaving a 2" (5 cm) lip on one flap as shown.

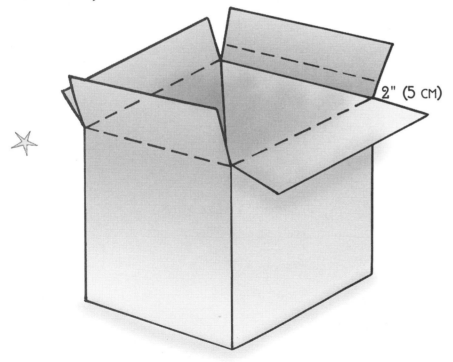

2" (5 CM)

2. Use the other box to make a false bottom and side for the first box. They should be ¹/₂" (1 cm) shorter on all sides than those of the bottomless box.

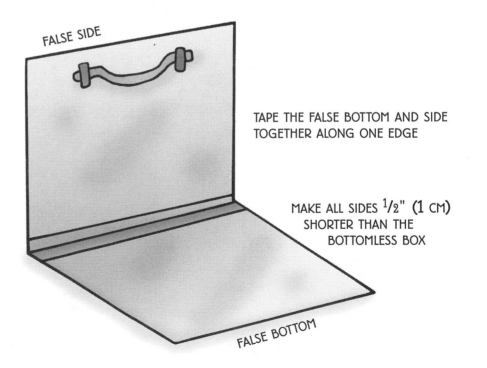

FALSE SIDE

TAPE THE FALSE BOTTOM AND SIDE
TOGETHER ALONG ONE EDGE

MAKE ALL SIDES ¹/₂" (1 CM)
SHORTER THAN THE
BOTTOMLESS BOX

FALSE BOTTOM

3. From the excess cardboard, cut out a cardboard handle. Tape it securely to the inside of the false side as shown.

4. Paint the inside of the box and both sides of the false bottom and side black; let dry.

Place the false bottom and side into the box and tape to the lip of the box as shown. The handle should be facing to the rear.

TAPE FALSE BOTTOM AND SIDE TO THE BOTTOMLESS BOX HERE

Finale Folder Trick

Every act needs an ending. You don't want to perform a trick and then just walk off the stage, so you need a "finish" — a way to let the audience know the show is over and it's time for that final round of applause. Here's a trick that will work well for your finale.

Props: finale folder (page 112), yarn or a little glitter in a shallow dish, table

The trick:

1. *"You'll really like this trick."*

Hold up the folders the long way with the flaps. The "The End" flap is to the front, the blank flap is to the back, close to your chest.

2. Let go of both front flaps so the folder falls open to show the inside of the blank folder. The folder with the writing inside is hanging down and hidden from the audience.

3. Cross your arms so the audience can see the back of the "blank" folder.

4. Unfold your arms and bring the folder back to its original position. Close up the folder.

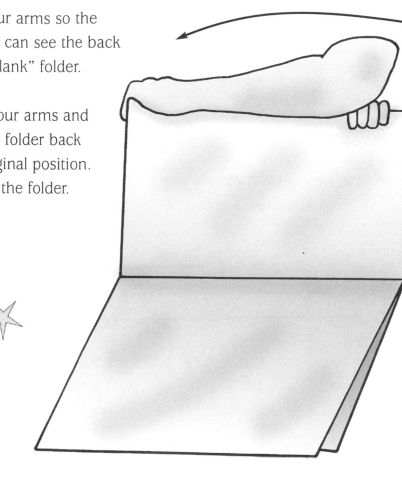

5. *"All I need is a little yarn (or glitter)."*

Pick up the yarn or glitter and slip it into the blank folder.

"A few magic words and we have …"

Release just the front flap and the folder falls open to show "The End."

Making the Finale Folder

You need: 2 same-color file folders, about 9$^1/_2$" by 11$^3/_4$" (23.5 x 29.5 cm); ruler; scissors; pencil, glue; yarn or glitter

To make the folder:

1. Trim both folders so the 9$^1/_2$" (23.5 cm) side measures 8" (20 cm). (This will remove the tabs on the top edges of the folders.)

2. Glue one folded side of each file folder together. Spread glue on both sections and press both sections together; let dry.

TRIM THESE EDGES TO 8" (20 CM)

GLUE THIS SECTION TO THIS SECTION

You now have two file folders that can be shown to the audience to look like one. If you open it up one way it looks like one file folder.

If you open it the other way, it still looks like one file folder.

3. Open up the file folder and lay it flat on a table. With the pencil, lightly write or print "The" on the top half of the folder and "End" on the bottom half of the folder. Glue along the pencil lines and press yarn or sprinkle glitter along the glue letters.

voila!

Getting Your Act Together

So now you know all of these amazing tricks. You've practiced and practiced and tried out your routines in front of pets and mirrors. You're ready to face an audience. Well then, it's time to take your show on the road!

What's Your "Magician Personality"?

The type of magic tricks you enjoy performing will help you determine what type of magician you'll enjoy being on stage. Do you like funny tricks like the MAGIC SHOPPING TRICK (pages 103 to 104)? Maybe you'll be a clown magician with a goofy outfit that makes everyone laugh. If you like big, flashy tricks, like the DISAPPEARING PERSON TRICK (pages 106 to 107), you could wear a bright, dazzling costume. Or perhaps you enjoy dressing the part of a character like a witch, a wizard, or a sorcerer such as Merlin the Magician or Harry Potter. There's always the traditional look with a white shirt, black cape, and top hat (page 115).

And if you just want to wear your everyday clothes and do simpler tricks, that's fine, too!

You should wear whatever fits your personality and makes you feel comfortable while you're performing. Yard sales and secondhand clothing stores are great places to look for inexpensive items for an outfit or costume.

Check out professional magicians, such as Lance Burton, David Copperfield, David Blaine, and The Amazing Jonathan, when they appear on TV and at their websites (page 123). It will give you ideas for your own look and style.

The Master Magician says ...

Abracadabra! You're ready! *Here's a fast, easy magician's outfit. All you need is a white T-shirt, a white painter's hat (available at a hardware store, it's like a baseball cap but made of paper-thin fabric), and fabric pens. Write your magician name on the shirt and hat. Then decorate them with designs or pictures.*

Making a Top Hat

You need: measuring tape, scissors, large sheets of black construction paper, glue, pencil

To make the hat:

1. Measure around your head. Add 2" (5 cm). If your head measures 18" (45 cm), for example, add 2" (5 cm) to make it 20" (50 cm). Cut a 9" (22.5 cm) strip of black construction paper in that length.

2. Roll the construction paper to make a cylinder 9" (22.5 cm) high. Overlap the edges by about 2" (5 cm) and glue them. Let dry.

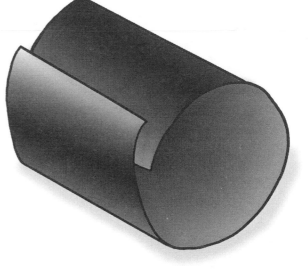

3. Cut 1" (2.5 cm) slits 1" (2.5 cm) apart along the bottom edge and the top edge.

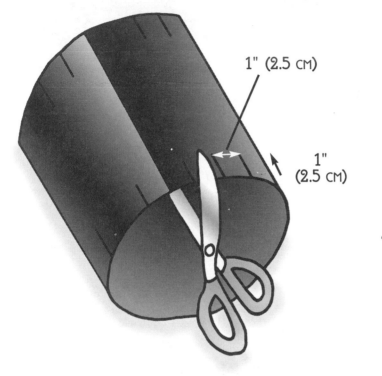

1" (2.5 CM)

1" (2.5 CM)

FOLD IN

4. Fold these slits facing out on the bottom and in on the top to make tabs.

FOLD OUT

5. Trace around the cylinder on another piece of construction paper. Make a circle 2" (5 cm) larger around the first traced circle.

Cut out the larger and smaller circles. Set aside the smaller circle. Trace the paper ring onto another piece of paper and cut out a second ring.

2" (5 CM)

6. Place the cylinder on a flat surface. Slide one of the paper rings down over the top of the cylinder. Glue the bottom tabs to the ring.

Glue the smaller circle to the tabs at the top of the cylinder. Let dry.

7. Turn the cylinder over. Glue the second paper ring to the underside of the first ring, hiding the tabs. Now you have a fancy high hat.

introducing...
THE LILLY
& BONZO
SHOW!!!

Planning Your Act

Start by making a list of all the tricks you know well enough to perform confidently in front of an audience. Group them into sets that you think would work well together in a routine (maybe they use similar props or it's easy to move smoothly from one to the other). Imagine yourself as a member of the audience and think about what you would find entertaining or funny. See my suggestions for Magical Mini-Routines on pages 26, 44, 64, 68, 71, and 90, too. Avoid doing four or five versions of a really similar trick, how-ever. Variety keeps things interesting — for you and for the audience!

Aim for a short 10- or 15-minute show. Reread the sections on Just Say the Magic Word! (page 8) and Keep That Patter Going! (page 8) and prepare a script for your act. Practice all of the tricks with the patter.

For your opening trick, choose a short attention-grabber. Here are a few quick tricks that would work well: the Coin from the Ear Trick (page 34), the Flick Knot Trick (pages 62 to 63), the Three Scarves in the Air Trick (pages 73 to 74), or any of the rubber band tricks (pages 26 to 32).

Choose a flashy trick for a finale, such as the Disappearing Person Trick (pages 106 to 107). The Finale Folder Trick (pages 110 to 111) is the perfect finishing touch. Don't forget to say "Thank You" and "I hope you enjoyed the show." Then bow to the thunderous applause!

presto!

The Master Magician says ...

Two routines are better than one!

Chances are, you'll read about new tricks that sound fun or you'll buy new props to try. After you've practiced them, add them to your routine. When you have enough new tricks, you can put together a whole new routine. It's always good to have have more than one, in case you perform for the same people.

Magician Jokes

Here are some funny, short jokes to work into your patter.

Waldo is a great magician. He was driving down the street and he turned into a gas station.

What do you get when you cross a chicken with a magician?
Cheep tricks.

Why did Waldo the Magician do well in school?
Because he was good at trick questions.

What do you get when you cross a bat with a magician?
A flying sorcerer.

What did the fishing magician say?
Pick a cod, any cod.

What do you get when you cross a snake with a magician?
Abraca cobra.

Why can't you do card tricks on a boat?
Because someone is sitting on the deck.

Have you seen Waldo the Magician's famous trick?
He makes a golf ball float. He drops a golf ball into a glass of root beer with two scoops of ice cream.

Taking requests! *Let's say someone in the audience asks for a specific trick. If you know it, go ahead and perform it — chances are it will be a new trick for the rest of the audience, and the person who requested it will probably have forgotten most of the details. You can also say, "Here's a very similar trick," and perform a different trick that uses the same prop.*

Organizing Your Props

You'll have to carry all of your props with you to wherever you are performing, so it's helpful to organize them in a plastic case or a large box (it keeps them tidy at home too!). Make a list of all the props you'll need for each trick and keep it in the case or box. Then just check them off as you're getting ready for a performance.

For the actual show, I recommend organizing each trick in a bag labeled with the trick name and numbered according to your routine, so you aren't fumbling through the box during the performance.

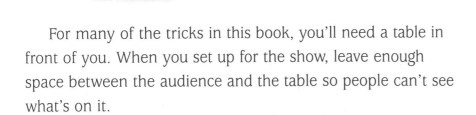

For many of the tricks in this book, you'll need a table in front of you. When you set up for the show, leave enough space between the audience and the table so people can't see what's on it.

Where to Perform

Two of the best places to do your first shows are at home in front of family and friends and in your classroom at school. This way you'll be performing for people you know and it won't be too scary.

Once you feel comfortable performing in front of a group with all eyes watching you, then you can try larger or unfamiliar audiences. Here are a few places that would probably welcome a magician:

- School or church functions

- Clubs or organizations you belong to, such as Scouts or the YMCA

- Clubs or organizations your parents belong to

- Talent shows that you might find listed in local newspapers or on community message boards

- Parties (a friend's or relative's birthday party, for example)

We All Make Mistakes ...

If a trick doesn't work or you flub up your patter, don't get flustered, you'll only make more mistakes. Slow down and concentrate on what you're doing. Have you let the secret out? Most people won't even notice. But if you think the trick won't work or you really messed up (and we all do at times), don't get nervous and start apologizing or trying to explain what went wrong. Just shrug your shoulders and say, "Whoops!" or "I'll have to practice that one a little more and get back to you." Put the trick away and move right on to the next one.

Here's a funny prop to keep handy (just in case). Paste a new cover over an old telephone book. The cover might say "No-Fail Magic" or "Tricks Made Easy." If you make a mistake, grab the book and flip through the pages. Stop at one page and read the instructions to yourself, mumbling and following along with your finger. Then tear out the page and crumple it up, saying, "Well, I'll never do that trick again."

✶ Got a Case of Stage Fright? ✶

At your first few performances, you might get what's called stage fright. Your knees and hands are shaky, your stomach is full of butterflies, and perhaps you forget the words to the opening trick. Take a deep breath, collect your thoughts, and go on with the show. As long as you've practiced your tricks enough, chances are, once you hear the first laugh or the first applause, your fears will disappear like magic! And it can't hurt to review WE ALL MAKE MISTAKES ... (above) before you go on.

All Eyes on ... You!

I've been entertaining people with my magic tricks for years. Here are my suggestions to help you put on a magic show that will have the audience calling for an encore!

- Here's the most important tip: Relax and try to smile when you are performing. That might be hard at the beginning because you'll be concentrating on a lot of things, but it will get easier. If the people in the audience see that you're enjoying yourself, they will enjoy themselves too.

- Be sure you have practiced enough. Don't add a trick to your routine until it's really ready.

- Hold your hands out in front of you at about shoulder height, when using a prop in your hands. Don't make it difficult for your audience to see what you're doing.

- Talk to your audience — not to your hands or down at the floor. This is especially true when you're doing tricks on a table. Learn the trick so well that you can look at and talk to your audience while you perform the trick.

- Go slow. Take your time. Don't rush to get through each trick.

- Speak slowly and clearly. Don't try to use a funny voice. Try to cut out bad speech habits such as "like," "you know," "um," "and so on" or other expressions that you might overuse.

- Oh, and did I remind you to practice?

- Don't forget: The whole point of magic is fun and enjoyment for you and for your audience. Relax! Smile! Enjoy!

The Magician's Resource Guide

Looking for more information on your favorite magicians, directions for tricks, props, and loads of ideas for costumes and routines?

Magic on the Web

Just type the word "magic" at your favorite search engine and you'll get millions of entries! Typing in "magic tricks" will get over half a million. Many top magicians have their own web sites: < **www.dcopperfield.com** > for David Copperfield; < **www.lanceburton.com** > for Lance Burton.

Magic Books and Magazines

Libraries and bookstores have many books on magic. There are others that are published by the magicians themselves, and these can be bought from magic supply stores (page 124).

Both of the clubs listed under magic clubs (page 124) have their own magazines, and there are also a few independent magicians' magazines.

GENII
The Conjurors' Magazine
4200 Wisconsin Ave. NW
Washington, DC 20016
202-363-4544

MAGIC
The Independent Magazine for Magicians
6225 Harrison Dr. Suite 4
Las Vegas, NV 89120
702-798-0099
www.magicmagazine.com

ABRA cadabra
Goodliffe Publications
150 New Road Bromsgrove B60 2LG
United Kingdom
http://user.itl.net/ ~ encore/abra.html

Magic Clubs

The Society of Young Magicians (SYM)
P.O. Box 510260 S
St. Louis, MO 63151
www.magicsam.com/sym
The SYM is for magicians ages 7 to 17. SYM's magazine is *Magic SYMbol*.

The International Brotherhood of Magicians
11137-C South Towne Square
St. Louis, MO 63123
314-845-9200
www.magician.org
Junior members ages 12 to 18 are accepted. This organization's magazine is *Linking Rings*.

Magic Camps and Classes

Want to hang out with fellow magicians? Many summer camps offer magic, and YMCAs and other organizations some-times offer magic classes during the rest of the year. Check your local papers, local bulletin boards, or the Internet.

Magic Supply Stores

To find a magic supply store near you, check the Yellow Pages. Look for magic stores, magician's supplies, or magic dealers. You can also check a local hobby shop or toy store for magic sets.

If you can't find supplies locally, there are many mail-order and online dealers. Here are some I have used:

Abbott's Magic Co.
124 St. Joseph St.
Colon, MI 49040
616-432-3235

David Ginn
4387 St. Michaels Dr.
Lilburn, GA 30047
770-923-1899
www.ginnmagic.com

Daytona Magic Shop
36 South Beach St.
Daytona Beach, FL 32114
904-252-6767

Hank Lee's Magic Factory
127 South St.
Boston, MA 02111
617-482-8749
http://magicfact.com/index.html
The greatest catalog I've ever seen —the size of a large city phone book! It makes great reading.

Ickle Pickle Products
808 Somerton Ridge Dr.
St. Louis, MO 63141
314-434-3630

La Rock's Fun & Magic Outlet
3847 Rosehaven Dr.
Charlotte, NC 28205
704-563-9300
www.larocksmagic.com

Louis Tannen, Inc.
24 West 25th St.
New York, NY 10010
212-929-4500
www.tannenmagic.com

Magic, Inc.
5082 North Lincoln Ave.
Chicago, IL 60625
773-334-2855

Samuel Patrick Smith Magic
P.O. Box 787
Eustis, FL 32727
353-365-7262
www.spsmagic.com

Silly Farm Products
2142 Tyler St.
Hollywood, FL 33020
954-923-4816

Index

More Good Books from Williamson Publishing

 Williamson's **Kids Can!**® books for ages 7 to 14 are each 128 to 176 pages, fully illustrated, trade paper, 11" x 8¹/₂", $12.95 US/$19.95 CAN.

The Kids' Book of
INCREDIBLY FUN CRAFTS
by Roberta Gould

Selection of Book-of-the-Month, Scholastic Book Club
KIDS COOK!
Fabulous Food for the Whole Family
by Sarah and Zachary Williamson

American Bookseller Pick of the Lists
Parents' Choice Approved
SUMMER FUN!
60 Activities for a Kid-Perfect Summer
by Susan Williamson

Parents' Choice Approved
Parent's Guide Children's Media Award
BOREDOM BUSTERS!
The Curious Kids' Activity Book
by Avery Hart and Paul Mantell

Parents' Choice Gold Award
Benjamin Franklin Best Juvenile Nonfiction Award
KIDS MAKE MUSIC!
Clapping and Tapping from Bach to Rock
by Avery Hart and Paul Mantell

HANDS AROUND THE WORLD
365 Creative Ways to Build Cultural Awareness
& Global Respect
by Susan Milord

Parents' Choice Approved
Dr. Toy Best Vacation Product
KIDS GARDEN!
The Anytime, Anyplace Guide to Sowing & Growing Fun
by Avery Hart and Paul Mantell

JAZZY JEWELRY
Power Beads, Crystals, Chokers, & Illusion and
Tattoo Styles
by Diane Baker

Parents Magazine Parents' Pick
Real Life Award
KIDS LEARN AMERICA!
Bringing Geography to Life with People, Places & History
by Patricia Gordon and Reed C. Snow

THE KIDS' MULTICULTURAL CRAFT BOOK
50 Creative Activities from 30 Countries
by Roberta Gould
full-color, $14.95

Parents' Choice Recommended
ForeWord Magazine Book of the Year Finalist
PAPER-FOLDING FUN!
50 Awesome Crafts to Weave, Twist & Curl
by Ginger Johnson

Parents' Choice Recommended
The Kids' Guide to
MAKING SCRAPBOOKS & PHOTO ALBUMS!
How to Collect, Design, Assemble, Decorate
by Laura Check

American Bookseller Pick of the Lists
Dr. Toy Best Vacation Product
KIDS' CRAZY ART CONCOCTIONS
50 Mysterious Mixtures for Art & Craft Fun
by Jill Frankel Hauser

Parents' Choice Gold Award
American Bookseller Pick of the Lists
THE KIDS' MULTICULTURAL ART BOOK
Art & Craft Experiences from Around the World
by Alexandra M. Terzian

American Bookseller Pick of the Lists
Skipping Stones Nature & Ecology Honor Award
EcoArt!
Earth-Friendly Art & Craft Experiences for 3- to
9-Year-Olds
by Laurie Carlson

Parents' Choice Approved
Benjamin Franklin Best Multicultural Book Award
THE KIDS' MULTICULTURAL COOKBOOK
Food & Fun Around the World
by Deanna F. Cook

Parents' Choice Recommended
Orbus Pictus Award for Outstanding Nonfiction
KIDS' ART WORKS!
Creating with Color, Design, Texture & More
by Sandi Henry

Teachers' Choice Award
Dr. Toy Best Vacation Product
CUT-PAPER PLAY!
Dazzling Creations from Construction Paper
by Sandi Henry

American Bookseller Pick of the Lists
Parents' Choice Recommended
ADVENTURES IN ART
Arts & Crafts Experiences for 8- to 13-Year-Olds
by Susan Milord

Parents' Choice Approved
KIDS CREATE!
Art & Craft Experiences for 3- to 9-Year-Olds
by Laurie Carlson

Benjamin Franklin Best Education/Teaching Gold Award
Parent's Guide Children's Media Award
HAND-PRINT ANIMAL ART
by Carolyn Carreiro
full color, $14.95

Early Childhood News Directors' Choice Award
Real Life Award
VROOM! VROOM!
Making 'dozers, 'copters, trucks & more
by Judy Press